new to cooking

new to cooking

simple skills and great recipes for fabulous food

lesley waters

photography by **peter cassidy**

RYLAND
PETERS
& SMALL

LONDON NEW YORK

Senior Designer Louise Leffler
Designer Emilie Ekström
Commissioning Editor Elsa Petersen-Schepelern
Editor Sally Somers
Production Deborah Wehner
Art Director Gabriella Le Grazie
Publishing Director Alison Starling

Food Stylist Julz Beresford
Assistant Food Stylist Annalisa Aldridge
Stylist Helen Trent
Photographer's Assistant Rachel Tomlinson
Indexer Hilary Bird

First published in Great Britain in 2001 by
Ryland Peters & Small
20–21 Jockey's Fields
London WC1R 4BW
www.rylandpeters.com

This paperback edition first published in 2005

10 9 8 7 6 5 4 3 2 1

ISBN 1 84172 829 2

A CIP record for this book is available from the
British Library.

Printed and bound in China.

Notes

All spoon measurements are level unless
otherwise noted.

All fruit and vegetables should be washed
thoroughly and peeled in the usual way, unless
otherwise advised.

Unwaxed citrus fruits and cucumbers should be
used wherever possible.

Soft cheeses and uncooked or partly cooked eggs
should not be served to the very old or frail, the very
young or to pregnant women.

Ovens should be preheated to the specified
temperature. Recipes in this book were tested with
a fan-assisted oven. If using a regular oven,
increase the cooking times according to the
manufacturer's instructions.

The publisher and author
would like to thank the following
companies and stores who
loaned the glassware, plates,
bowls, cutlery, table linen
and accessories that appear
in the book:

Purves & Purves
220–224 Tottenham Court Road
London W1T 7QE
020 7580 8223

The Conran Shop
81 Fulham Road
London SW6 6RD
020 7589 7401 for stores

Heal's
196 Tottenham Court Road
London W1T 7LQ
020 7636 1666 for stores

Dedication
For Barbara and Mac

Author's acknowledgements
Many thanks to my friends, neighbours and family
who chomped their way through this book. To Sally
Somers for patiently (and politely!) checking and
rechecking and for Peter Cassidy's thoroughly
modern and fresh approach to the photography.
Last, but certainly not least, Annalisa Aldridge and
Emma Marsden for their hard work and dedication
in the kitchen.

contents

6   good food is for every day...

the kitchen
8   tools and utensils
9   storecupboard basics
10 menu planning
11 tips and techniques

12 the basics
14 boiling
24 poaching
30 steaming
36 microwaving
40 stir-frying
48 frying
54 deep-frying
60 grill pans
66 barbecues
74 grilling
78 roasting
86 braising
94 baking

102 the recipes
104 eggs
112 salads
119 soups
123 fish and seafood
128 chicken and duck
135 meat
139 vegetables
143 dressings, dips and sauces
146 sweet things
154 drinks

158 index

good food is for every day...

I meet a lot of people who want to cook but don't know how or are too scared to enter the kitchen in case they make a mistake. To me the most important things about cooking are confidence, enjoyment and not being afraid to make mistakes. In fact, they can often be put right to give even better results – some of the best recipes started life by accident!

I have been cooking for over twenty years now, and for eight of those I was a cookery teacher. Of all the work I've ever done – whether it was writing books or presenting on TV, or working in a restaurant – this was my most fulfilling time. Seeing people become liberated in a kitchen was so exciting, and giving them the confidence to make lovely food was just such a pleasure.

My dream is to have a cookery school – and perhaps this book is the first stepping stone. I heard someone say the other day, 'Good is simple, simple is good', which sums up perfectly how I feel about food and the way it is now.

When I was training to be a chef, many of the recipes were very, very complicated and often rich and over garnished. Since then my style of food has changed dramatically. I believe that good food is for every day and not once every two weeks for a dinner party. Don't put this book on the shelf and dip into it only once in a while – use it every day! To me, real cookbooks are those which are well thumbed and splattered with ingredients.

This is the book that will teach you the skills that you will use every day, without unnecessary complications. I'll teach you how to make simple bread but tell you to buy the sponge fingers to go in your Peach Marsala Trifle – life really is too short, and cutting a few corners doesn't have to mean compromising on taste.

New to Cooking will show you how to have fun and success in the kitchen. The opening chapter is dedicated to essential utensils and important storecupboard ingredients. Next are the chapters which teach you the basic techniques – from poaching, steaming and baking to roasting and grilling – all illustrated with modern recipes to guide you along the way.

I know it's tempting to go straight to the recipes and to get cooking, but do read the tips at the beginning of all the 'Basics' chapters first – they contain lots of essential information.

Once you've got all the basics under your belt, the second part of the book is graduation time, with fabulous recipes for you to put the skills into practice.

I'm often asked what my favourite style of food is and it's always a difficult question to answer. All I can say is that I've been inspired by all the different people I have met and the places I have been – they have all contributed to the way I cook and eat now. I hope this book can be the beginning of your inspiration.

the kitchen

On these pages is a simple list of essential equipment and storecupboard basics and how to store them. If you already have some of these items, take all your equipment out of the cupboards and drawers and lay it on the table. Then check the tools list to see if you have everything, and put it in its place. If there's any equipment left on the table and you haven't used it in the last 12 months, give it to a friend or to a charity. As funds allow, try to assemble all the equipment in the Startup Kit. For Christmas and birthdays, perhaps your friends can be persuaded to give you the items on the Wish List.

The storecupboard is the backbone of your cooking and enables you to be spontaneous in the kitchen. There are many dishes that can be prepared using storecupboard

basics. However, being well-stocked doesn't mean bulk-buying. It means choosing ingredients which you will need on an everyday basis.

As well as a stock of basics such as beans, pasta and rice, it's also a good idea to keep your favourite flavourings, to turn something ordinary into something special.

tools and utensils

Startup kit
For a basic set of equipment, buy the best you can afford, then they'll last.

In Your Cupboards

1 non-stick frying pan
1 non-stick wok with lid
1 heavy shallow pan with ovenproof handles for stove-top or oven cooking
3 saucepans – small, medium and very large – with lids
1 collapsible metal steamer, bamboo steamer or 2-tier steaming saucepan
1 wire rack
1 hand-held blender
1 sieve (strainer)
1 colander with legs or stand
1 box grater
1 set of plastic bowls
1 measuring jug
1 lemon squeezer
1 salad spinner

On the Shelf

1 set of measuring scales
salt and pepper mills
1 cafetière and/or 1 teapot

In a Block or Wrap

1 paring or utility knife
1 large chopping knife
1 bread knife
1 pair kitchen scissors
1 sharpening steel

On the Work Surface

1 heavy wooden chopping board
1 white heavy plastic board for raw meat and fish
1 roll of kitchen paper

In a Large Utensil Pot

2 wooden spoons
1 large metal spoon
1 large slotted metal spoon
1 ladle
1 potato masher
1 long handled turner (fish slice)

2 plastic spatulas
1 set salad servers
1 pair of tongs

In the Top Drawer

1 potato peeler
1 can opener
1 corkscrew
2 metal skewers
1 rolling pin

In the Bottom Drawer

greaseproof paper
aluminium foil
non-pvc food wrap
1 roll medium freezer bags
1 roll of large heavy-duty black bin bags
1 roll of kitchen string
tea towels
apron
oven gloves

For the Oven

1 non-stick roasting tin
12-hole non-stick muffin tin
1 non-stick baking sheet

Wish list
Put these desirable objects on your 'wish list' for Christmas and birthdays.

In Your Cupboards

1 food processor
1 electric mixer
1 stove-top grill pan
6 ramekin dishes (150 ml)
3 glass bowls – small, medium and large
1 rolling pin
1 cooking thermometer
1 olive oil drizzler
1 mortar and pestle
1 mini blender

In a Large Utensil Pot

extra wooden spoons
1 metal whisk
1 palette knife
1 meshed spoon for deep-frying

In the Top Drawer

bakewell paper
1 roll large freezer bags
1 pastry brush

In the Bottom Drawer

more tea towels (12 total)
another apron
another set of oven gloves

For the Oven

another non-stick roasting tin
1 loose-bottomed flan ring
   (25 cm diameter)
1 non-stick springform cake
   tin (20 cm diameter)
1 cake tin (18 cm square)
another non-stick baking sheet

storecupboard basics

Startup kit

For every day, when there's just you, cook whatever you fancy and serve it however you wish.

Staples

2–3 packets pasta, various
   shapes
2–3 packets rice – long grain,
   basmati, Thai fragrant,
   risotto
egg or rice noodles
dried lentils (Puy are my
   favourites)
plain and self-raising flour
baking powder
coffee, tea and sugar

Cans and Cartons

vegetable bouillon (stock)
chicken bouillon (stock)
cans of: chopped tomatoes,
   chickpeas, cannellini and
   borlotti beans, anchovies in oil
coconut cream or milk

Oils and Vinegars

large bottles of olive oil and
   sunflower oil
small bottles of extra virgin
   olive oil for salads, peanut
   oil for frying, chilli oil for
   flavour
balsamic vinegar
Worcestershire sauce
red and white wine vinegar

Spices

whole nutmegs
ground cumin
ground coriander
ground turmeric
ground cinnamon and
   cinnamon sticks
sweet paprika
crushed dried chillies

Seasonings and Flavourings

coarse sea salt
black peppercorns
soy sauce (light and dark)
Tabasco
teriyaki sauce
smooth Dijon mustard
runny honey
vanilla essence

Fresh Foods

a bag of onions
a head of garlic
2–3 red chillies
fresh ginger
fresh herbs, such as parsley
carrots
potatoes
tomatoes
lemons, limes, oranges, apples
   and pears

In the Refrigerator

eggs
milk
unsalted butter
a wedge of Parmesan cheese
feta cheese
Greek yoghurt

In the Freezer

vanilla ice cream
frozen peas
ice cubes

Extra items

When you've got the basics, start to add these extra ingredients for more adventurous cooking.

Staples

couscous or cracked wheat
strong white bread flour
easy-blend dried yeast
jumbo oats
sultanas or raisins
cocoa powder
caster sugar
muscovado sugar

Oils and Vinegars

small bottles of sesame oil
   and walnut oil

Spices

saffron threads

Seasonings and Flavourings

Thai fish sauce
horseradish sauce
tomato chutney
wholegrain Dijon mustard
English mustard powder
sun-dried tomatoes and
   peppers
black olives
capers
red wine
brandy
Marsala or sherry

Fresh Foods

your choice of other herbs,
   such as chives, basil, thyme
   and rosemary

menu planning

For everyday, when there's just you, cook whatever you fancy and serve it however you wish.

However, if you're entertaining, menu planning isn't hard – there are just a few basic principles to keep in mind.

number of courses

• Decide on the number of courses – three is common (first, main and pudding). Two is fine also (a main course and something else).

• However, you can add extras – before-dinner snacks, salads, cheese and chocolates after!

• Serving cheese. The French do it before the pudding, the English after, and the Americans serve it any time. Please yourself! Just an idea – if you serve cheese after the main course, you can drink the same wine you had with that.

• Serving salads. Mostly, salad is served after the main course, as a palate cleanser. But you can also have it with the cheese (cheese and leaves are great together) or as a very healthy first course. You can even make an especially big one and have it as the only course for lunch.

balance

• Serve only one cheesy dish in a meal – if you had goat's cheese salad for first course, don't serve cheese later.

• If you had a cream sauce with the main course, don't serve cream or ice cream with the pudding.

• If you had pastry or eggs in your first course, don't have them for a main course or pudding.

• If you had seafood for first course, don't have fish for main – unless of course you have a serious passion for oceanic eating!

• Don't make every course a hot one. People like the contrast of something chilled – and it makes life easier for you, the cook.

colour and texture

• Don't have three courses of pale food. If you have chicken, don't have potato and leek soup. For main course, make sure only one vegetable is white – if you are serving potatoes, for example, avoid serving cauliflower at the same time.

• People like contrasting textures. So if you're having mashed potatoes, don't have another mashed or puréed vegetable. Make the others crunchy.

• But don't make everything crunchy either.

presentation

• Keep it simple.

• When adding a garnish, only add something that's relevant to the dish, and make sure it is edible. So if you've used parsley in the dish for flavouring, garnish with parsley.

• Don't put too much on the plate at once. Think of the rim around the plate as the frame of a picture, and only put food inside the frame.

making life easy

• Make sure at least one course can be prepared a day ahead or in the morning. Braises, tarts (savoury or sweet) and ice cream can all be prepared ahead.

• Make sure you've got room – in the kitchen, in your oven, in the refrigerator, even on the table. Wash up as much as you can before you serve the meal, clear away all the ingredients as you use them to leave room for you to work. It all helps to make life easy.

• Don't ask too many people, or you make life difficult for yourself.

allergies

• When you ask people to dinner, ask them if there's anything they can't eat. They may be allergic, or have religious taboos. Common allergies include shellfish, crustacea, fish and nuts. They may be vegetarians – and if they're vegans, they won't be able to eat eggs or dairy foods either.

drinks

• Serve your favourite wines, and don't worry about rules like white wine with white meat and red with red meat.

• Tastes vary, but reckon on about ¾ bottle per person, and ask your friends to bring a bottle.

• With Asian food, I suggest beer or Gewürztraminer wine.

• Always have lots of mineral water, still and sparkling.

tips and techniques

deseeding tomatoes

Halve the tomatoes crossways. Squeeze one half gently in one hand. Using the fingertips of your other hand, scrape out the seeds and pulp. Repeat with the remaining half.

lemon and lime juice

To get maximum juice from lemons or limes, roll them up and down on a board with the palm of your hand, pressing down as you roll, before squeezing them.

toasting nuts and seeds

Heat a dry frying pan over a high heat, then add the nuts or seeds in a single layer. Cook for about 1 minute, turning often with a spoon, shaking the pan lightly to move them around, until toasted. Remove the pan from the heat and tip the seeds or nuts onto a cold plate – don't leave them in the pan, or they will carry on toasting until they burn. When toasting larger nuts, spread them out on a baking tray and cook in a hot oven. Toast for about 5–6 minutes until golden.

chopping herbs

Don't over-chop herbs, or they lose much of their flavour and fragrance. Using kitchen scissors or a very sharp knife, give them just a few chops.

making parmesan cheese shavings

Take a wedge of fresh Parmesan and, using a swivel potato peeler, pull lightly down the side of the cheese towards you to make curls.

cooking dried beans

Personally, I always use canned beans, but if you would like to use dried ones, soak them overnight in cold water to cover, then drain, put in a saucepan, bring to the boil and simmer until tender (up to 2 hours, depending on the age of the beans). Never add salt at the beginning of cooking, or the beans will be tough. Add 10 minutes before the end.

check the use-by dates

Clear out your cupboards regularly. Check use-by dates and throw away anything you know you won't use. Herbs and spices go stale and lose flavour, so buy small quantities and replace them often. Keep in a cool, dark place out of direct sunlight.

safety notes

Be conscious of food safety – food poisoning can be serious.

• Try to keep tea towels for drying clean dishes only, and use kitchen paper for food preparation. If you wipe your hands on a tea towel after handling meat, possible infections can easily spread.

• If cooking previously frozen food, defrost it properly before heating.

• Keep uncooked food refrigerated until you need it – don't leave it hanging around in the kitchen or garden in warm weather.

• Be patient. Never serve sausages, pork, chicken or turkey before they are completely cooked.

• Never put cooked food onto a plate that has had raw meat, poultry or fish on it.

the basics

First things first. Use these chapters to become familiar with all the different methods of cooking. Read the introductory tips in each section and try out the recipes, following the steps to master the techniques.

boiling

Cooking food in a saucepan of boiling water is simple and easy. Just think of all the familiar things you can cook in this way; boiled eggs, pasta and noodles, rice, potatoes and vegetables. It's a fat-free cooking method that preserves the green colour of vegetables and keeps the grains of rice and strands of pasta separate.

boiling tips

- Always fill the saucepan with lots of water – enough to cover the food completely – then bring it to the boil.

- Start with cold water for 'old' potatoes, chickpeas, beans and lentils, and boiling water for new potatoes, vegetables, noodles, pasta and rice.

- Lid on or off? Keep the lid off for long grain rice, pasta, noodles, green vegetables and new potatoes – put the lid on for other kinds of rice, 'old' potatoes and other root vegetables.

- If the lid is on, keep it slightly ajar, or the pan will boil over.

- For variations on boiling, see Poaching (page 24) and Braising (page 86).

blanching, refreshing and par-boiling

- Blanching means partially cooking foods, especially vegetables, by dunking them briefly in boiling water. This is especially good for green beans and broccoli, when you want a good, crunchy salad or if you are going to stir-fry the vegetables afterwards. Drain as soon as they turn a bright green, then refresh (see below).

- Refreshing is when the blanched food is plunged into iced water to stop it cooking and to set the colour. Drain again when it's cold.

- Par-boiling is when the foods, often vegetables, are half cooked by boiling in order to be finished by some other cooking method, often roasting. Par-boiling potatoes and parsnips before roasting them stops them drying out or shrivelling before they are roasted and cooked through.

classic creamy mashed potatoes

Choose large 'old' potatoes – the sort that become fluffy when mashed. Buy a good potato peeler – the kind with a swivel blade. These are very simple, old-fashioned utensils and, for some reason, they become sharper with age. When boiling potatoes, it's always important to add salt before cooking.

1 kg large 'old' potatoes, such as baking potatoes, peeled and cut into 5 cm cubes
about 150 ml milk, preferably hot
40 g butter
salt and freshly ground black pepper

serves 4

1 Put the potatoes in a medium saucepan. Add cold water to cover and a pinch of salt.

2 Bring to the boil, reduce the heat, cover with a lid and simmer for 15–20 minutes until tender when pierced with a knife. Drain and return the potatoes to the pan.

3 Return the saucepan to the heat and mash the potatoes with a fork or potato

masher for 30 seconds – this will steam off any excess water.

4 Stir in the milk and butter with a spoon.

5 Mash until smooth, adding extra milk if needed and salt and pepper to taste. Serve immediately, in a serving bowl or straight onto dinner plates.

classic creamy mashed potatoes

crushed herb mash

In this recipe, the potatoes are lightly crushed rather than mashed – they shouldn't be smooth. The garlic is cooked in the potato water until very soft, then crushed with the potatoes.

750 g large 'old' potatoes, cut into 2.5 cm cubes
4 garlic cloves, peeled
4 tablespoons extra virgin olive oil
½ teaspoon grated lemon zest
a bunch of basil, leaves torn
salt and freshly ground black pepper

serves 4

Put the potatoes and garlic into a saucepan, add a pinch of salt and cover with cold water. Bring to the boil, reduce the heat, cover with a lid and simmer for about 12 minutes until tender when pierced with a knife.

When the potatoes are nearly cooked, put the oil in a small saucepan, add the lemon zest and heat gently for 1 minute. Add the basil and heat for a further 20–30 seconds until it turns bright green.

Drain the potatoes and garlic and return them to the pan. Add the infused oil and salt and pepper to taste. Using a potato masher or fork, gently crush the potatoes, garlic and oil. Serve immediately.

flavoured mashed potatoes

Add extra flavourings to the basic mashed potato recipe opposite:

mustard mash Add 2 tablespoons English mustard and 3 tablespoons chopped parsley at the same time as the milk and butter.

sun-dried tomato mash Add 2 tablespoons sun-dried tomato paste, 50 g freshly grated Parmesan cheese and 3 tablespoons chopped basil at the same time as the milk and butter.

horseradish mash Add 3–4 tablespoons creamed horseradish sauce at the same time as the milk and butter. Serve sprinkled with chopped dill.

Mashed potato tips

• Best for mashing are large 'old' potatoes (often called floury or baking potatoes). They become light and fluffy when boiled.
• Cut them into evenly sized pieces, so they will cook at the same rate and all be ready at the same time.
• Always start them in COLD water. Bring to the boil, then simmer – with the lid slightly ajar – until tender when pierced with the point of a knife.
• Never use a food processor to mash your potatoes – you'll end up with wallpaper glue!

spring vegetable vinaigrette

The vegetables in this recipe are blanched and refreshed in iced water (page 15) to bring out their lovely bright colour and snappy texture. Have the bowl of iced water ready and, as soon as the vegetables are blanched, transfer them straight into the iced water. I think of this dish as a real celebration of spring, so prefer to use fresh peas, but if you can't find them, frozen will do instead.

125 g asparagus spears

125 g mangetout

125 g sugar snap peas

125 g shelled fresh peas

3 tablespoons olive oil

1 garlic clove, thickly sliced

salt and freshly ground black pepper

1 lemon, cut into wedges, to serve

serves 4

Using a small, sharp knife, trim off about 1 cm from the stalk end of the asparagus spears. Cut the trimmed spears in half lengthways.

Bring a large saucepan of water to the boil. Meanwhile, fill a large bowl with ice and cold water, so that it is ready to refresh the vegetables as soon as they are cooked. Add the asparagus, mangetout and sugar snap peas to the boiling water. Cover and return to the boil, then remove the lid and add the peas. Boil for a further 30 seconds.

Drain the vegetables, then tip them into the iced water to refresh.

Meanwhile, put the oil and garlic in a small saucepan and heat gently for 1 minute, to infuse. Remove the garlic and discard.

Drain the vegetables well, then spread sheets of kitchen paper on a work surface. Put the vegetables on top and let them dry off a little. Transfer them to a large serving plate and pour over the infused oil. Sprinkle with plenty of salt and pepper and serve with lemon wedges.

new potato salad with gazpacho dressing

Gazpacho is the famous Spanish chilled soup, made with tomatoes, peppers, onions and garlic. Use the same ingredients to make a fresh dressing for this simple salad of new potatoes. Add the dressing to the potatoes while they are hot, even if you aren't eating them straight away, as this will help the flavours to infuse.

500 g baby new potatoes, scrubbed but not peeled

gazpacho dressing

2 large, ripe tomatoes, halved, deseeded (page 11) and diced

50 g preserved roasted red peppers (in a jar), diced

½ small red onion, chopped

1 garlic clove, chopped

3 tablespoons extra virgin olive oil

2 teaspoons red wine vinegar

a pinch of sugar

a bunch of flat leaf parsley, coarsely chopped

salt and freshly ground black pepper

serves 4

Bring a large saucepan of water to the boil, add the potatoes and return to the boil. Reduce the heat and simmer for about 12 minutes or until the potatoes are just tender when pierced with a knife.

Meanwhile, put the dressing ingredients into a large bowl and mix well. Add plenty of salt and freshly ground pepper.

Drain the potatoes thoroughly and tip them into the dressing. Mix well and serve hot or let cool to room temperature.

Boiling green vegetables

• *Plunge them into a saucepan of BOILING water (never cold).*

• *Boil them with the lid off – this preserves some of the nutrients and bright colour. It also prevents them going soggy.*

• *Refresh in iced water as described on page 15, if using in cold dishes. If serving hot, serve straight away.*

Cooking new potatoes

• *New potatoes are firm and waxy, perfect for salads, or for serving whole, tossed in butter.*

• *Cook them unpeeled, or rub off their thin skins with a cloth.*

• *Plunge them into a saucepan of BOILING water (never cold) and simmer, with the lid off, until done.*

new potato salad with gazpacho dressing

simple spaghetti with capers and olives

Don't be tempted to add oil to the pasta cooking water – it is a myth that it stops pasta sticking – and is a waste of good oil! Just make sure you stir occasionally with a wooden fork or spoon while it is cooking.

375 g dried spaghetti
6 tablespoons virgin olive oil
2 garlic cloves, finely chopped
2 tablespoons capers, drained and
    rinsed, plus a few caperberries
    (optional)
12 kalamata olives, pitted and
    coarsely chopped
freshly squeezed juice of ½ lemon
8 tablespoons coarsely chopped
    flat leaf parsley
salt and freshly ground black pepper
fresh Parmesan cheese shavings
    (page 11), to serve (optional)

serves 4

Cook the spaghetti in a large saucepan of boiling, salted water, as directed on the packet, until cooked, or 'al dente'.

While the spaghetti is cooking, gently heat the oil in a small saucepan. Add the garlic and cook for 1 minute. Add the capers, olives and lemon juice and cook for a further 30 seconds. When the pasta is cooked, drain and return it to the warm pan. Add the caper mixture and parsley and toss well to coat. Add freshly ground black pepper and Parmesan shavings, if using, and serve.

penne with cheese, parma ham, spinach and rocket

Drain penne really well, because the water gets caught in the tubes.

375 g dried penne
2 egg yolks
125 g mascarpone cheese
50 g Parmesan cheese, freshly grated
50 g baby spinach leaves
50 g wild rocket
½ tablespoon extra virgin olive oil
8 slices Parma ham, each torn
    into 3 pieces
salt and freshly ground black pepper

serves 4

Cook the penne in a large saucepan of boiling, salted water, as directed on the packet, until cooked, or 'al dente'.

While the pasta is cooking, put the egg yolks, mascarpone and Parmesan in a bowl and mix well. Add plenty of black pepper.

Put the spinach, rocket and oil into a large bowl. Toss well, adding black pepper to taste.

When the pasta is cooked, drain and return it to the warm pan. Put the pan over a low heat and add the mascarpone mixture. Stir for about 30 seconds to mix. Divide the pasta between 4 pasta bowls, top each with a handful of rocket and spinach and finish with the Parma ham. Serve immediately.

Boiling pasta

• Bring a large saucepan of water to the boil, then add the pasta.
• Boil with the lid off and keep it boiling until the pasta is cooked.
• To test whether it's cooked, remove a piece with tongs, then bite it. It should be soft, but still slightly firm to the bite. This is called 'al dente', which literally means 'to the tooth' in Italian.
• Follow packet directions and taste often.

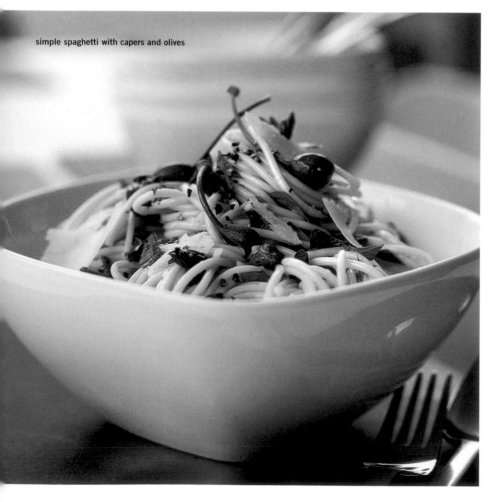

simple spaghetti with capers and olives

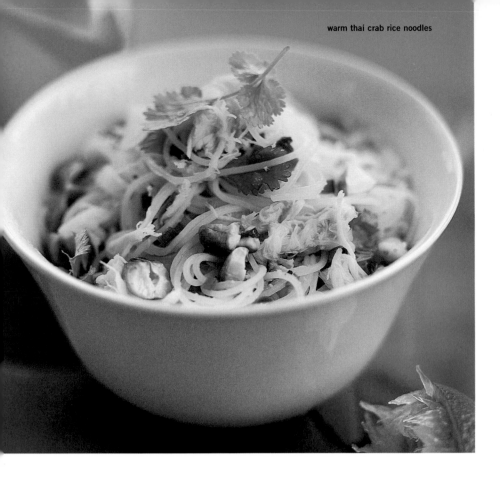

chillied chive egg noodles

Egg noodles are made with egg and wheat flour, and there are thick and thin kinds. They take longer to cook than rice noodles (made from rice flour) or beanthread noodles (made from mung bean flour).

250 g dried egg noodles
50 g butter
2 tablespoons chilli oil
a large bunch of chives,
   coarsely chopped
juice of ½ lemon
salt and freshly ground black pepper

serves 8 as an accompaniment

Cook the noodles in a saucepan of boiling water until tender, about 5 minutes, or as directed on the packet. Drain, rinse in cold water and set aside.

Heat the butter and oil in a large saucepan or wok until hot. Add the noodles and toss until heated through. Add the chives and lemon juice and toss well to coat. Add salt and pepper to taste and serve at once.

warm thai crab rice noodles

Rice noodles cook very quickly, so be careful not to overcook them. Rinsing them in boiling water removes excess starch and keeps them in strands, not clumps.

250 g dried rice noodles, preferably thin
340 g canned white crabmeat, drained,
   or 200 g fresh

dressing
2 tablespoons sunflower oil
1 medium red chilli, finely chopped
1 medium green chilli, finely chopped
2.5 cm piece of fresh ginger, peeled
   and finely chopped
grated zest of 1 lime and juice of
   2 limes
1 tablespoon Thai fish sauce
leaves from a large bunch of coriander
50 g cashew nuts, lightly toasted
   (page 11)
salt and freshly ground black pepper

serves 4 as starter, light lunch or supper

Soak or cook noodles as directed on the packet. Meanwhile, boil the kettle and put the crabmeat into a large bowl.

To make the dressing, put the oil in another bowl. Add the chillies, ginger, lime zest and juice, fish sauce and coriander. Stir, then add to the bowl of crabmeat. Add salt and pepper to taste.

When the noodles are cooked, drain and rinse with the kettle of boiling water. Return the noodles to their bowl or saucepan, then add half the crab mixture and half the cashew nuts. Toss well.

Divide the noodles between 4 plates and top each with a spoonful of the remaining crab mixture. Sprinkle with the remaining nuts and serve.

Boiling noodles
• Cook in the same way as pasta, but don't add salt to the cooking water, because this will mask their flavour.
• Add salt AFTER cooking. If adding soy sauce or fish sauce – the salts of Asia – you won't need to add salt as well.
• Rinse cooked rice noodles in boiling water to stop them from sticking together.

cardamom and orange buttered rice

Start testing a few grains of rice before it should be done, and keep checking as it cooks – that way, you won't overcook it.

10 cardamom pods
375 g long grain rice
2 fresh bay leaves
a large strip of orange zest
25 g butter
salt and freshly ground black pepper

serves 4

Split open the cardamom pods, discard the shells, and lightly crush the seeds with a mortar and pestle. Alternatively, put the seeds on a board and use the back of a spoon to crush them lightly.

Bring a large saucepan of water to the boil. Add the rice, bay leaves, orange zest and cardamom seeds. Return to the boil, reduce the heat to a simmer and cook with the lid off for about 12 minutes until the rice is just cooked. Drain well through a sieve.

Return the pan to the heat and add the butter. When melted, add the rice, stir well, add salt and pepper to taste and serve.

Boiling rice
• Cook long grain rice in a large saucepan and plenty of boiling water, until tender but still with a slight bite in the middle, about 12–15 minutes, with the lid off.
• To cook basmati and Thai fragrant rice, rinse to remove the starch, put in a large saucepan and add cold water to 2.5 cm above the rice level. Cover with a lid and bring to the boil, reduce the heat and simmer until the water is absorbed, about 5 minutes. Remove the pan from the heat and let stand, with the lid on, for about 10 minutes until cooked.

smoky puy lentils with balsamic vinegar and pancetta

Chickpeas and beans need presoaking before boiling. However, lentils do not, so this is a quick and easy dish. Do keep an eye on them as they cook as they can dry out quickly and may need extra boiling water added.

5 red peppers, quartered lengthways
  and deseeded
3 large red onions, cut into
  8 wedges each
8 tablespoons olive oil
500 g Puy or brown lentils, rinsed
3 tablespoons balsamic vinegar
6 unpeeled garlic cloves
125 g pancetta or streaky bacon, diced
salt and freshly ground black pepper

serves 4

Preheat the oven to 200°C (400°F) Gas 6.

Put the peppers and onions into a large roasting tin. Pour over 3 tablespoons of the oil and add plenty of salt and pepper. Roast in the preheated oven for 30 minutes.

Meanwhile, to cook the lentils, put them into a large saucepan and add 1 litre (twice their volume) of cold water. Bring to the boil, remove the lid and cook at a fast simmer until the water has been absorbed and the lentils are tender, about 20–25 minutes.

Put the remaining oil and balsamic vinegar into a small bowl and whisk well. Add the garlic and pancetta or bacon to the onions and peppers and roast for 15 minutes more or until golden. Remove from the oven.

Squeeze the insides of the roasted garlic out of their skins into the balsamic dressing and mix. Drain the cooked lentils and put them into a large bowl. Pour in the dressing, add salt and pepper to taste and stir through.

Add half the roasted vegetables and pancetta to the lentils, stir gently, then transfer to a serving dish. Spoon the remaining vegetables and pancetta or bacon on top and serve.

thai fish broth

poaching

Poaching is a gentle way of cooking and is a variation of boiling. The cooking liquid is brought to the boil, then the heat is reduced so the liquid is barely trembling, with few bubbles breaking the surface. It is a good way of cooking delicate foods, such as fish or eggs, which break up when boiled – or chicken, which becomes tough when boiled. In China and South-east Asia, poaching is done in a wok.

poaching tips

- Poach in simmering, not boiling, liquid. It should be barely trembling when the food goes in.

- To get to simmering, boil the liquid in a saucepan or wok with the lid on. Remove the lid, reduce the heat and wait for the bubbles to subside.

- Add the food carefully to the liquid and always poach with the lid off, to let the steam escape.

- Use a slotted spoon to remove food from its poaching liquid. If you are keeping the liquid, for example when it is stock, drain through a sieve or colander into a bowl.

liquids for poaching

- You can poach in any liquid – water, stock (chicken, fish or vegetable), milk or coconut milk.

- Water is the most basic poaching medium – as it is flavourless, you need to season it well before adding the food.

- Chicken or vegetable stock is good for chicken, which will have a richer flavour. In Asian cooking, fish, also, is often cooked in chicken stock.

- Milk: bring it almost to the boil – take care because it boils over easily. This is good for poaching fish, especially smoked fish.

- Coconut milk: bring it almost to the boil – if it boils it will curdle. This is used for Asian dishes.

poaching eggs

- Poaching is a classic way to cook eggs.

To poach an egg, bring a deep saucepan of lightly salted water to the boil. Add 1 tablespoon white wine vinegar and reduce the heat to a simmer. Crack the egg into a cup and swirl the water with a fork to create a whirlpool effect. Slide the egg into the water. Cook for 3 minutes, then remove with a slotted spoon. Sit the spoon on a piece of kitchen paper on a plate, let drain for 10 seconds, then serve.

thai fish broth

Thai curries often use the poaching method. It is a good way to cook the delicate flesh of fish and seafood and the poaching liquid becomes the sauce or broth. Thai curry pastes are easy to make, but you can also buy them. Pastes vary in heat, so taste first — you'll need 2–3 tablespoons.

about 600 ml vegetable stock

400 g canned coconut milk

375 g salmon fillet, cut into chunks

250 g uncooked tiger prawns, peeled but with the tails on

125 g sugar snap peas, halved lengthways

2 tablespoons basil leaves, torn

freshly squeezed juice of 1 lime

freshly ground black pepper

cooked Thai fragrant rice (page 22), to serve

thai curry paste

1 tablespoon oil

4–5 tablespoons of the coconut milk

5 cm fresh ginger, peeled and chopped

1 green chilli, halved, deseeded and chopped (page 43)

1 red chilli, halved, deseeded and chopped (page 43)

1 tablespoon chopped lemongrass

1 teaspoon coriander seeds

1 shallot, chopped

1 garlic clove, chopped

1 teaspoon salt

serves 4

1 To make the Thai curry paste, put all the paste ingredients into a blender or food processor and blend briefly.

2 The texture should be a coarse paste.

3 Heat a wok over medium heat, add the paste and stir-fry for 2 minutes. This will release the flavours of the spices. ⇨

Poaching in coconut milk

• *If coconut milk boils, it 'splits' (curdles).*

• *Bring it to just below boiling, then reduce the heat until barely simmering.*

• *Canned coconut cream won't curdle, so use it if available.*

• *Don't worry too much if it does curdle (Asian cooks don't).*

4 Add the stock.

5 Add the coconut milk and heat to simmering, so that the liquid is just moving.

6 Add the salmon and prawns. Bring back to simmering, then cook for 2 minutes.

7 Add the sugar snap peas. Cook for a further 1 minute until the fish is just cooked (it will be opaque all the way through).

8 Add half the basil leaves and salt and pepper to taste, then stir. Add the lime juice and sprinkle with the remaining basil leaves. Spoon a share of rice into each bowl, ladle the broth over the top, then serve.

wholegrain mustard tarragon chicken

Chicken is excellent poached in stock – the result is rich but healthy. Keep the leftover stock in this recipe to use another time.

4 large sprigs of tarragon
2 litres chicken or vegetable stock
4 boneless, skinless chicken breasts
125 g salad leaves
crusty bread, to serve

mustard dressing
4 tablespoons extra virgin olive oil
1 teaspoon wholegrain mustard
salt and freshly ground black pepper

serves 4

Strip the tarragon leaves from the stalks, reserve the leaves and put the stalks and the stock into a large saucepan. Cover with a lid and bring to the boil, then remove the lid and reduce the heat to a very gentle simmer, so the stock is barely moving.

Put the chicken breasts between 2 pieces of clingfilm and, using a rolling pin, bash and flatten each piece to 1 cm thickness. Remove and discard the clingfilm.

Put the flattened chicken pieces into the stock and poach gently for about 12–15 minutes until firm to the touch and cooked through, with no trace of pink in the middle. Drain and let cool a little, reserving the stock for another recipe. (Keep refrigerated for up to 3 days or freeze it.)

Meanwhile, coarsely chop the tarragon leaves and put in a mini-blender. Add the dressing ingredients and 1 teaspoon water and blend for 1–2 minutes until smooth.

Slice the chicken diagonally into finger-size strips. Divide the salad leaves between 4 large plates and top with the slices of chicken. Drizzle with the dressing and serve immediately with crusty bread.

Poaching in stock
• *Poaching in stock will add flavour to the food being cooked in it.*
• *You can use chicken or vegetable stock for chicken, but you don't have to use fish stock for fish – you can also use chicken stock, vegetable stock or milk.*

steamed sweet baby carrots with
orange and coriander

Steamed food is cooked by trapped vapour from heated liquid. An indirect form of heat, it may be created in a saucepan, in a foil parcel, or by a tray of water in the oven. The food is cooked by moist heat and retains all its juices and flavours. If you like fat-free cooking, this is one of the methods for you.

pan-steaming

- Set a perforated steamer over simmering water in a saucepan, wok or frying pan.

- Half-fill the pan or wok with water – there should be enough not to boil dry, but it should not reach the food, or it will boil, not steam.

- Add the food to the steamer only once the water has come to the boil, then cover the pan with a lid to trap the steam.

- To steam fish, line the perforations with a cloth (muslin) to stop it sticking or breaking up.

Steamers available include:

- A collapsible perforated plate on little legs (see left) which can be put into any saucepan or pan, and the food arranged on top.

- A metal saucepan-steamer set, with a steamer like a second saucepan with holes in the bottom.

- Chinese bamboo steamers.

- Other utensils can also be used – try a colander or metal sieve set over a pan of boiling water.

foil-steaming

- Cut out a square of foil, put the food in the middle, fold so the foil overlaps on top, then scrunch the edges of foil together to seal.

- Cook in a steamer, in the oven or on a barbecue. The food will be cooked by the steam trapped inside the foil.

oven-steaming

- Put small ovenproof dishes in a roasting tin.

- Pour boiling water to reach half way up the sides of the dishes, then cover the whole tin tightly with foil, to trap the steam.

- Put the tin in a preheated oven to cook.

steaming

steamed sweet baby carrots with orange and coriander

This is the simplest form of steaming and a good way to cook many vegetables, such as broccoli, cauliflower and beans. They cook to perfection in the steamy heat — healthy and delicious! If you don't have a special steamer, use a colander or sieve set over a pan of boiling water instead.

500 g baby carrots, halved lengthways
a strip of orange peel
freshly squeezed juice of 2 oranges
15 g butter
1 teaspoon caster sugar
a pinch of salt
2 tablespoons coarsely chopped coriander leaves
freshly ground black pepper

serves 4

Put about 2 cm water in a large saucepan. Cover and bring to the boil over a high heat. Put the carrots into a metal or bamboo steamer or colander and put into or over the pan. Reduce the heat and simmer for 5–8 minutes, or until the carrots are just tender.

Meanwhile, put the orange peel, juice, butter, sugar and salt into a small saucepan. Heat until boiling, then reduce the heat and simmer gently for about 5 minutes until reduced by half. Remove and discard the orange peel.

Put the steamed carrots into a serving dish. Add the coriander and orange mixture and toss well. Add plenty of black pepper and serve.

steamed mussels with garlic and vermouth in a foil parcel

When you make a parcel of foil, the vermouth turns to steam and cooks the mussels in a delicious scented vapour. Let everyone open their own parcel — as they open it up, the scented steam smells heavenly.

1 kg mussels, in their shells
50 g butter
150 ml dry vermouth
2 garlic cloves, crushed

to serve
crusty bread
a bunch of flat leaf parsley, coarsely chopped (optional)

4 pieces of foil, about 60 x 30 cm
1 baking sheet

serves 4

Preheat the oven to 200°C (400°F) Gas 6.

Scrub the mussels clean and rinse them in several changes of cold water to remove grit. Pull off the beards or seaweed-like threads and discard any mussels that are cracked or that don't close when tapped against the kitchen counter — these are dead and not edible.

Fold each piece of foil in half lengthways and divide the butter, vermouth, garlic and mussels between them. Bring the corners of each piece together to close each parcel, leaving a little space in each one so the mussels with have room to open. Pinch the edges of the parcels together to seal.

Put the parcels on a baking sheet and transfer to the preheated oven. Cook for 10–12 minutes or until all the mussels have opened — check by opening one of the parcels.

Put the parcels on heated plates and serve with crusty bread to mop up the delicious juices.

If you like, put coarsely chopped parsley in a bowl and serve separately for people to sprinkle over their mussels when they open the parcels.

Steaming fish in a wok
• Method 1: Cover the bottom of a wok with water, add a plate, upside down, so it doesn't touch the water. Put the fish on top, cover with the wok lid and heat until steaming.
• Method 2: Put a plate in a bamboo steamer, add the fish and flavourings, then steam in the usual way. The fish won't break up, and the flavourings will seep into the flesh.

steamed mussels with garlic and
vermouth in a foil parcel

Cooking in a steam bath

• *Cooking food in dishes set in a roasting tin of hot water is a very gentle way of cooking. It is often used for egg dishes, so the eggs won't overheat and curdle.*

• *The steam bath is called a bain-marie.*

lime and ginger honey puddings

Putting dishes in a tray of hot water creates a bain-marie. It produces a gentler heat than direct oven heat, and makes for lighter results.

2 tablespoons runny honey
3 pieces stem ginger, finely chopped
1 tablespoon stem ginger syrup
grated zest and juice of 2 limes
85 g butter, softened (room temperature)
85 g caster sugar
2 eggs, beaten
85 g self-raising flour
double cream or vanilla ice cream,
  to serve

4 ramekin dishes, buttered
a roasting tin, for the bain-marie

serves 4

Preheat the oven to 200°C (400°F) Gas 6.

1 Put the honey, ginger and syrup into a bowl, add the juice of 1½ limes and mix well.

2 Put the ramekins in a roasting tin and divide the mixture equally between them.

3 Put the butter and sugar into a bowl and whisk until light and fluffy. Gradually add the beaten eggs, whisking all the time.

4 Sift the flour into the mixture, add the lime zest and remaining lime juice and fold in (mix gently) with a large metal spoon.

5 Spoon on top of the honey and ginger mixture, dividing the mixture equally between the ramekins.

6 Pour enough boiling water into the tin to come half way up the sides of the ramekins.

7 Cover the whole roasting tin with foil and seal tightly around the edges.

5

6

7

8

8 Transfer to the preheated oven and cook for about 40 minutes until soft and springy on top and a cocktail stick inserted in the middle comes out clean.

Run a knife round the edges to loosen, turn out onto plates and serve hot with cream or ice cream.

microwaving

The microwave oven uses intense heat created by high-speed waves to cook food very quickly. It is good for cooking green vegetables, fish and steamed puddings. It's a handy stand-by, but should never be considered as an oven in its own right.

microwave tips

- Don't lose the instruction booklet that comes with your microwave. For successful microwave cooking, always follow the manufacturer's instructions to the letter.

- Never put metal in any form into your microwave. This includes roasting tins, foil or crockery with gold or silver leaf. Metal damages the oven.

- Plastic, ovenproof glass, ceramic or special microwave dishes are best.

- If using clingfilm, buy special microwave-safe brands. It should be vented at one corner. Don't use with the browning unit – it will melt.

- Cover the food with a lid, plastic or a saucer or plate, but check if the covering should be loose, otherwise the food may boil over and splatter your oven.

- Smaller, evenly sized foods will take less time to cook than one large piece. If cooking jacket potatoes, they will cook more evenly if you arrange them in a circle.

- Wipe out the oven with a damp cloth every time you use it.

- Don't salt the food before microwaving or it may dry out or become tough.

- Let dishes stand for a few minutes after microwaving to distribute the heat evenly.

- Always check food half-way through cooking time. The heat is very powerful and food may take less time to cook than you think. Some dishes also need stirring half-way through the cooking time.

microwave strengths

Microwaves are especially good for:

- Cooking vegetables, such as broccoli and carrots.

- Steaming firm white fish (such as cod) if you are short of time.

- Making quick sponge puddings.

- Softening butter.

- Melting chocolate.

- Heating up leftovers.

broccoli trees with pan-fried pine nuts

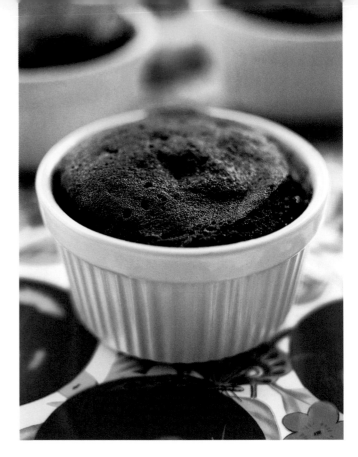

Microwave settings

• Microwave ovens vary in wattage, or strength. These recipes have been tested in a 750 watt oven. If yours is less than that, allow more time. Always check the instruction booklet.

• Recipe books and prepacked foods will give power levels, such as HIGH or MEDIUM. These levels equal:

HIGH – 100 per cent
MEDIUM-HIGH – 70 per cent
MEDIUM – 50 per cent
MEDIUM LOW – 30 per cent
LOW – 10 per cent

• Different ovens cook at different speeds, even at the same wattage, so test the food just before the end of cooking time.

broccoli trees with pan-fried pine nuts

This is about as speedy as good cooking gets! Broccoli is ideal for the microwave, as the stalks and florets cook evenly and don't go soggy.

500 g broccoli
25 g butter
50 g pine nuts
salt and freshly ground black pepper

serves 4

Cut the broccoli into medium florets, leaving a long stalk. Put into a large, microwave-safe bowl, add 50 ml water, cover with microwave-safe clingfilm or a lid and microwave on HIGH for 3 minutes.

Meanwhile, put the butter, pine nuts and salt and pepper to taste in a small saucepan over medium heat. Cook for 2–3 minutes until the nuts are golden and the butter is foaming.

Drain the broccoli through a colander or sieve, return to the bowl and toss with the pine nuts and butter. Serve immediately or let cool and serve as a salad.

warm chunky fish pâté

Flake the cooked fish into big pieces — this shouldn't be a smooth pâté.

150 g salmon fillet, skin on
150 ml white wine
125 g cream cheese
4 tablespoons Greek yoghurt
2 tablespoons coarsely chopped dill
a squeeze of fresh lemon juice
salt and freshly ground black pepper

to serve
black rye bread, toasted
1 lemon, cut into wedges

serves 4

Put the salmon, skin side up, in a shallow microwave dish. Add the wine and cover with microwave-safe clingfilm. Cook on MEDIUM for 5 minutes.

Meanwhile, put the cream cheese, yoghurt, dill and lemon juice in a large bowl and mix.

Drain the fish on kitchen paper and flake into large pieces. Gently fold the fish into the cream cheese mixture and season to taste.

Serve with bread or toast and lemon wedges.

saucy chocolate pots

These gooey puddings show how versatile the microwave can be.

100 g mascarpone or cream cheese
115 g muscovado light brown sugar
25 g cocoa powder
2 eggs
1 teaspoon vanilla essence
40 g self-raising flour
thick cream, to serve

4 ramekins, 150 ml each, buttered

serves 4

Put all the ingredients into a large bowl or food processor. Beat with an electric whisk or process until blended. Divide the mixture among the ramekins.

Cover each ramekin loosely with microwave-safe clingfilm. Put 2 of the ramekins, spaced well apart, on the microwave tray and cook on HIGH for 1 minute 15 seconds. Let stand with the clingfilm on while you microwave the remaining 2 pots. As soon as the second 2 pots are cooked, remove the clingfilm from the first 2. Let the second 2 stand for 2 minutes. Remove the clingfilm and serve with thick cream.

honey teriyaki vegetables

Stir-fried food is cooked in an open pan or wok over a high heat. It is a healthy, fast way to cook, using only minimal oil. The food is constantly moved around a large surface area of hot pan and cooks evenly and quickly. A wok is absolutely ideal for stir-frying and, of all the pans in my kitchen, it's probably the one that I use the most.

which wok?

- Buy a wok with a lid, so you can also use it for making soups and stews, or steaming (page 30).

- Non-stick woks are ideal and can be used for all sorts of dishes, including big batches of scrambled eggs and super-thin omelettes.

- If you have an electric stove top, choose a wok with a flat bottom.

- If you don't have a wok, a large frying pan can be used instead.

wok cooking tips

- Have all the ingredients prepared and ready – stir-frying is a speedy process, and you won't have time to peel and chop once you start.

- Chop vegetables or meat into evenly sized pieces so that they all cook at the same rate.

- Heat the wok or pan first before adding any oil, to prevent the oil from burning.

- Stir-fry over a high heat – the food must be cooked quickly to be crunchy.

- Don't walk away! Stir the food constantly with a wooden spatula or wok scoop to keep it moving and cooking evenly. Food falls down the sides to the hottest part of the wok in the centre, so keep stirring and flipping the food.

- Don't be tempted to put too much food into the wok or pan at one time, as this reduces the temperature and makes vegetables soggy rather than crunchy.

stir-frying

hot wok chilli prawns with cucumber coriander salsa

honey teriyaki vegetables

Teriyaki is a Japanese glaze, made from sake or mirin (rice wines), shoyu (Japanese soy sauce) and sugar. You can buy these ingredients in large supermarkets or Eastern food stores.

2 teaspoons peanut oil

a bunch of radishes, washed, trimmed and halved lengthways

4 carrots, sliced diagonally

a bunch of spring onions, halved crossways

125 g mangetout, halved lengthways

1 tablespoon sesame seeds, toasted (page 11), to serve

dressing

1 tablespoon runny honey

2 tablespoons teriyaki sauce

freshly ground black pepper

serves 4

To make the dressing, put the honey and teriyaki sauce in a small bowl and mix. Add black pepper to taste.

Put the oil in a wok and heat until hot. Add the vegetables and 2 tablespoons water and stir-fry for about 3 minutes, until the vegetables are just heated through but are still crisp. Transfer to a warm serving dish.

Reduce the heat and return the wok to the heat. Add the dressing and heat it through gently until just warm. Drizzle the dressing over the vegetables, sprinkle with the sesame seeds and serve.

hot wok chilli prawns

Fast stir-frying is great for seafood, which mustn't be overcooked.

1 red chilli

500 g peeled, uncooked tiger prawns, with the tails on

grated zest and juice of 1 lime

1 garlic clove, chopped

2 tablespoons sunflower oil

a pinch of sugar

cucumber coriander salsa

½ cucumber

a bunch of coriander

1 tablespoon rice vinegar

1 teaspoon sugar

salt and freshly ground black pepper

serves 4

1 To prepare the chilli, cut it in half lengthways, scrape out the seeds and discard.

2 Cut each half lengthways into fine strips.

3 Cut the strips crossways into very fine dice. ⇨

4 Put the prawns into a bowl and add the chilli, lime zest and juice, garlic, 1 tablespoon of the oil and the sugar.

5 Using a potato peeler, remove the peel from the cucumber.

6 Cut the peeled cucumber into slices lengthways, then stack the slices and cut them into strips.

7 Cut the strips crossways into dice.

8 Coarsely chop the coriander.

9 Put the cucumber and coriander into a second bowl, add the rice vinegar and sugar, then mix, adding salt and pepper to taste.

10 Heat the remaining sunflower oil in a wok over high heat and add half the prawn mixture.

11 Stir-fry for 1–2 minutes until pink and cooked. Keep them warm in a very low oven while you stir-fry the remaining prawns.

12 When cooked, divide the prawns and cucumber coriander salsa between 4 plates and serve.

stir-fried pork in lettuce cups

The pork is stir-fried first, then braised – a typical Chinese cooking method.

500 g pork mince
1 tablespoon peanut oil
1 red pepper, halved, deseeded and
 finely diced
2 garlic cloves, crushed
a bunch of spring onions, finely sliced
 with the green tops reserved
3 tablespoons dry sherry
3 tablespoons soy sauce
6 tablespoons oyster sauce
crisp inner leaves from 1 iceberg
 lettuce, halved
leaves from a bunch of coriander
freshly ground black pepper
hoisin sauce, for dipping

serves 4–6

Heat a dry wok until hot, add the pork mince and cook for 3–4 minutes until opaque. Remove to a plate with a slotted spoon.

Wipe out the wok. Add the oil and heat. Add the pepper, garlic and spring onion and cook for 2 minutes. Add the pork and stir-fry for a further minute. Add the sherry and cook for 1 minute.

Stir in the soy and oyster sauces and bring to the boil. Reduce the heat and simmer for 8–10 minutes until the liquid has almost evaporated. Add plenty of black pepper.

Spoon the pork mixture into the lettuce leaf cups and sprinkle with the coriander and reserved spring onion tops. Serve with the hoisin sauce for dipping.

hot chicken tikka platter with yoghurt

If you have two woks, use both for this. Otherwise, you can use a large frying pan and a wok.

3 boneless, skinless chicken breasts,
 cut into strips
juice of 1 lemon
4 tablespoons tikka or mild curry paste
2 garlic cloves, crushed
250 g French beans
1 tablespoon oil
125 g baby spinach leaves
freshly ground black pepper

to serve

a bunch of coriander, coarsely chopped
 (optional)
150 g Greek yoghurt

serves 4

Put the chicken strips into a large bowl and sprinkle with the lemon juice. Add the tikka or curry paste and garlic. Mix well. (If time allows, chill and marinate for 30 minutes.)

Heat a large wok or frying pan. Add the chicken with its marinade and cook for 5–7 minutes until the chicken is opaque throughout. Add black pepper to taste.

Meanwhile blanch the beans (page 15) in boiling water. Heat a second wok or large frying pan. Add a tablespoon of oil and, when hot, add the drained beans, remove from the heat and add the spinach leaves. Toss to mix.

To serve, pile the spinach and beans into the centre of a large serving dish. Top with the hot chicken, sprinkle with coriander, if using, and serve with Greek yoghurt.

hot chicken tikka platter with yoghurt

frying

Frying is cooking food in an open frying pan with the aid of fat such as butter, oil or a mixture of both. Omelettes, eggs, meats and vegetables are all quickly cooked this way.

frying tips

- Preheat the pan before you add the oil, so that the base of the pan heats evenly.

- Preheat the oil in the pan before adding any food – it should sizzle as it touches the pan. If it's not hot enough, the food will absorb too much oil.

- Don't put a lid on the pan when frying – the food will steam, not fry, and be soggy rather than crisp.

- Don't crowd the pan. Adding too much food at once will lower the temperature of the oil and steam the food. Fry in batches, and keep them warm in the oven while you cook the next batch.

- Put enough oil in the pan for the food to cook evenly on both sides, allowing for some of the fat to be absorbed. This also avoids a tide mark on foods such as fishcakes.

- Don't overheat the oil or heat it for too long. It will break down, start to smoke and taint the flavour.

- Drain fried food on kitchen paper and eat it while it is still hot and crisp.

non-stick pans

- I prefer non-stick pans – buy the best you can afford, the heavier the better.

- Remember, don't overheat the pan, use 'kind' utensils, such as wood, be gentle when washing them (don't use scourers) and store hanging up.

choosing oil

- Olive oil is healthier and tastes great (don't fry in extra virgin – save it for salads and finishing foods).

- Peanut and sunflower oil have little flavour, so use them when you don't want any added taste (for example, when cooking Asian foods).

- When frying in butter, always use unsalted butter, and add a splash of oil to stop it burning (butter burns at a lower temperature than oil).

herby potato rösti

Frying creates the lovely crispy crust that's essential for rösti.

3 large potatoes, peeled
3–4 large sage leaves
a sprig of thyme, leaves stripped
4 tablespoons olive oil
salt and freshly ground black pepper

serves 6

1 Grate the potatoes on the coarse side of a box grater and dry well on kitchen paper.

2 Finely chop the sage and thyme leaves, discarding any woody stalks.

3 Put the grated potato in a bowl, add the herbs and mix well.

4 Using your hands, shape a heaped tablespoon of the mixture into a ball.

5 Heat half the oil in a large frying pan until hot. Add the shaped potato cake to the pan and flatten with a long-handled turner.

6 Shape 2 more potato balls, add to the pan, flatten with the turner and fry for 5 minutes until golden.

7 Turn the rösti over and lower the heat. Continue to cook for 5–10 minutes until golden and cooked through. Transfer to a very low oven to keep them warm. Repeat with the remaining mixture.

Transfer to a serving plate, sprinkle with salt and pepper and serve immediately.

fried tomatoes with green pistou

Frying quickly in a very small quantity of oil, as in this recipe, is known as sautéing, from the French word 'to jump'. I think sautéing is more like stir-frying, but don't toss these tomatoes around too much or they'll break up. Pistou is the French version of pesto – in France it is a herb mix traditionally stirred into soup, but here it is served as a fragrant accompaniment to the crisp-coated tomatoes.

4 large plum tomatoes
50 g polenta
½ teaspoon salt
olive oil, for frying
fresh Parmesan cheese shavings (page 11), to serve

pistou
50 ml extra virgin olive oil
2 garlic cloves, coarsely chopped
a large bunch of basil
salt and freshly ground black pepper

serves 4

To make the pistou, put the oil, garlic and basil into a small food processor and process until blended. Add salt and pepper to taste.

Cut each tomato crossways into 5 slices and discard the top and bottom slices.

Put the polenta onto a plate, add the salt and mix. Dip the tomato slices into the polenta to coat and transfer to a clean plate.

Put ½ cm oil in a frying pan and heat until hot. Add the tomato slices and fry for 1–2 minutes on each side until the polenta is lightly golden. Remove, drain on kitchen paper and sprinkle with salt.

Put 3 tomato slices on each plate, slightly overlapping. Spoon around the pistou, top with the Parmesan shavings, sprinkle with freshly ground black pepper and serve hot.

gremolata pork with lemon spinach

This recipe demonstrates one of the great advantages of shallow-frying. Foods can be coated in breadcrumbs, polenta, or other crumbly things, then fried gently to give a crisp outside and tender inside.

4 boneless pork chops, 75 g each
1 tablespoon basil oil
50 g ciabatta bread, torn into pieces
4 tablespoons coarsely chopped flat leaf parsley
grated zest of 1 lemon
2 tablespoons olive oil
freshly ground black pepper

lemon spinach
250 g young spinach, washed, dried and finely sliced
1 tablespoon extra virgin olive oil, plus extra for serving
freshly squeezed juice of ½ lemon

serves 4

Trim any excess fat from the pork chops, leaving a thin layer around the meat. Put each chop between 2 pieces of clingfilm and, using a rolling pin, beat to ½ cm thickness.

Remove and discard the clingfilm and put the pork in a bowl. Add the basil oil and sprinkle with black pepper. Turn to coat, cover and refrigerate for 2 hours.

To make the breadcrumbs, put the ciabatta pieces into a food processor and pulse to coarse crumbs. Put the breadcrumbs, parsley and lemon zest into a bowl and mix. Add black pepper to taste. Transfer to a plate and coat the pork with the crumb mixture, pressing gently until coated on both sides.

Heat the oil in a large frying pan, add the pork and cook for about 2–3 minutes on each side or until the breadcrumbs are golden and the pork is cooked through.

Meanwhile, put the spinach in a large bowl, add the olive oil and lemon juice and toss to coat.

Put a mound of spinach on each plate and top with the pork. Drizzle with the olive oil, sprinkle with freshly ground black pepper and serve.

Deep-fried food is cooked by completely immersing in very hot oil. Done properly, it doesn't have to mean greasy fish and soggy chips – deep-fried food, from chips to tempura, should be light and sizzling. Follow these tips for perfect results.

Deep-frying tips

- Deep-fry in a large saucepan, deep fryer or wok.

- Do not fill the pan more than half full with oil.

- Use either sunflower or peanut (groundnut) oil or vegetable oil. These can all be heated to very high temperatures.

- Use fresh oil every time – used oil has impurities that affect the flavour of the food.

- Don't add too much food to the pan at once – this lowers the temperature of the oil and stops a crisp shell forming. It might also make the pan overflow. The larger the pieces, the fewer should go in at once.

- Do not cover the pan – this creates steam, which stops the food from becoming crisp.

- Tip fried food onto kitchen paper to drain off the excess oil. Sprinkle immediately with sea salt for savoury foods, or sugar for sweet – to absorb excess fat and stop the food from tasting greasy.

Frying heat

- If you don't have a cooking thermometer, test the heat of the oil by adding a cube of bread. If it browns in:

  60 seconds, 180°C (360°F), it's suitable for gentle frying, such as the first stage of cooking chips.
  40 seconds, 190°C (375°F), for moderately hot frying.
  20 seconds, 195°C (385°F), for hotter frying, the right temperature for tempura and the second frying of chips.
  10 seconds. This means it's too hot! Turn off the heat immediately.

Safety rules

- Don't leave the pan unattended at any time – very hot oil needs to be watched carefully.

- Keep a heavy metal pan lid nearby in case the oil catches fire. If this does happen, turn the heat off immediately and slam on the lid.

deep-frying

salmon tempura with chilli sauce

salmon tempura

Tempura batter shouldn't be smooth, so mix it very briefly, using chopsticks rather than a fork. Make the batter just before you use it.

2 eggs
150 ml ice-cold sparkling mineral water
115 g plain flour
55 g cornflour
3 tablespoons finely chopped chives
500 g salmon fillet, sliced crossways into
   16 finger strips
sunflower oil, for deep-frying

chilli sauce
6 tablespoons sesame seeds, toasted (page 11)
3 red chillies, finely diced
2 tablespoons dark soy sauce
1 tablespoon white wine vinegar
1 tablespoon runny honey

serves 4

1 To make the sauce, put the sesame seeds and chillies in a bowl and add the soy sauce.

2 Add the vinegar and honey. Stir.

3 To make the batter, crack the eggs into a bowl.

4 Pour in the sparkling water and mix quickly.

5 Add the flours and stir briefly with chopsticks. Don't overmix – the batter should have lumps.

6 Add the chives and stir briefly. ⇨

7 Pour the oil into the deep-fryer, saucepan or wok and heat.

8 To test the heat of the oil, add a cube of white bread. If it browns in 20 seconds, the oil is ready for cooking. If you have a cooking thermometer, it should reach 195°C (385°F).

9 Dip the salmon pieces into the batter.

10 Add the pieces to the pan, 3 at a time, and fry, in batches, for 2–3 minutes until golden.

11 Remove from the oil, drain on kitchen paper and sprinkle with salt. Serve immediately with the chilli sauce.

Tips for frying in batter

• If making tempura (Japanese) batter, mix the batter at the very last moment, and mix it roughly so there are still quite a lot of lumps in it.

• To make other batters, follow the recipe, mix well, then set aside for about 30 minutes to allow the starch cells in the flour to expand – this will make the batter lighter.

• The Indian version of tempura is called bhaji or pakora – this batter contains gram flour made from chickpeas.

Electric deep-frying machines

• If you plan to deep-fry often, a deep fryer takes the guesswork out of oil temperatures. The machine heats the oil to the temperature you want, then automatically switches off.

• One of their advantages is that they fry with the lid on, which stops frying smells escaping.

• Always follow the manufacturer's instructions.

root vegetable chunky chips with coriander mayo

Perfect chips are cooked twice, at two different temperatures – first to cook them through, then in hotter oil to make them crisp and golden.

375 g sweet potatoes, cut into thick chips
375 g potatoes, cut into thick chips
375 g parsnips, cut into thick chips
sunflower oil, for frying
salt, to serve

coriander mayo
a large bunch of coriander, chopped
4 tablespoons mayonnaise
a squeeze of fresh lime juice
salt and freshly ground black pepper

serves 4

Soak the vegetable chips in a bowl of cold water for 10 minutes to remove excess starch. Drain and dry well with a tea towel.

Meanwhile, put the coriander and mayonnaise into a small food processor, add 1 tablespoon water and process until blended. Add the lime juice and salt and pepper to taste.

Half fill a deep-fryer or large saucepan with oil and heat to about 180°C (360°F), or until a cube of bread browns in about 60 seconds. Working in 2–3 batches, plunge the vegetable chips into the oil and cook for 6–8 minutes, until cooked through but not golden. Remove and drain on kitchen paper.

Increase the heat to about 195°C (385°F), or until a cube of bread browns in 20 seconds. Plunge the chips back into the oil and cook for 2–3 minutes until golden.

Remove, drain on kitchen paper and sprinkle with salt. Serve at once with coriander mayo.

Chip frying tips
• *Cut the potatoes into chips, then soak in water for 10 minutes to remove the starch. Drain and pat dry on kitchen paper.*
• *Fry chips in batches, to make sure the temperature of the oil remains constant.*
• *Fry first at 180°C (360°F) for 6–8 minutes.*
• *Drain on crumpled kitchen paper, then increase the heat to 195°C (385°F) and fry until crisp and golden – the time will depend on the size of the chips, but 2–3 minutes is a guide.*

grill pans

A stove-top grill pan is a ridged cast iron pan used on top of the stove to produce the intense, char-grilled flavours of a barbecue. This simple tool is definitely one of my favourite ways of cooking – the heat of the pan sears the outside of food and cooks it through quickly. It's also a healthy way to cook, since the food sits on the ridges above the fat and not in it.

Grill pan tips

- Always preheat the stove-top grill pan, then add the food when it is very hot.

- Brush the food – not the pan – lightly with oil before cooking, to prevent sticking.

- When you have added the food, don't move it around. When it is ready to turn, it will come away easily from the pan without sticking.

- Serve straight from the pan. If left to cool, meat will toughen and vegetables will continue to cook and become soggy.

- Marinating food first with oils, herbs and spices enhances the flavour.

- Salt food after cooking not before – salt draws out the moisture and can give dry results.

- Delicate white fish and salmon will cook quickly, but to make sure they cook all the way through reduce the temperature a little.

- For thicker foods, such as chicken, put a weight on top to ensure even contact with the pan. A saucepan half-filled with water works well.

seared scallops with brittle parma

Seared food is cooked quickly over high heat to seal the outside and form a nice crust. Scallops cook fast, and carry on cooking off the heat, so keep a careful watch on them – when overcooked, they are tough.

4 slices Parma ham
12 large scallops
125 g salad leaves such as lamb's lettuce
freshly ground black pepper

to drizzle
extra virgin olive oil
balsamic vinegar

serves 4

1 Heat a stove-top grill pan until very hot. Add the ham and cook for 1–2 minutes on each side until crisp. Remove and set aside.

2 Grind black pepper over the scallops.

3 Add the scallops to the hot pan. Cook for 1–2 minutes on each side until opaque.

4 Divide the salad leaves between 4 plates.

5 Lightly drizzle with oil.

6 Drizzle with a little balsamic vinegar.

Top the salad with 3 scallops, then break over the brittle Parma ham. Sprinkle with pepper and serve at once.

seared scallops with brittle parma

pan-grilled bruschetta with onion marmalade and goats' cheese

Char-grilled bread is more than just toast – it stays chewy on the inside, has a smoky flavour and lovely stripes from the grill pan.

2 ciabatta rolls, halved crossways
4 large handfuls of mixed salad leaves
1 tablespoon extra virgin olive oil, plus extra for serving
4 tablespoons red onion marmalade (page 145)
125 g soft, mild goats' cheese
salt and freshly ground black pepper

serves 4

Heat a stove-top grill pan until hot. Add the ciabatta and cook for 1–2 minutes on each side until lightly toasted and charred.

Meanwhile, put the salad leaves in a bowl, add the olive oil and salt and pepper to taste.

Spread the onion marmalade on the toasted ciabatta and put onto serving plates. Add a handful of salad and crumble the goats' cheese on top. Sprinkle with olive oil and lots of black pepper.

pan-grilled bruschetta with onion marmalade and goats' cheese

lamb steaks with coriander cumin crust

Lamb, like duck, can throw off quite a bit of fat as it cooks. The grill pan keeps the meat up and out of the fat, which you can just pour off as it accumulates.

1 tablespoon cumin seeds
1 tablespoon coriander seeds
1 tablespoon cracked black pepper
4 tablespoons flat leaf parsley, coarsely chopped
4 lamb steaks, from the leg, 150 g each
1 tablespoon olive oil
200 g Greek yoghurt
3 tablespoons mint leaves, chopped
1 teaspoon freshly squeezed lemon juice
salt and freshly ground black pepper

serves 4

Crush the cumin and coriander seeds coarsely with a mortar and pestle or the back of a wooden spoon. Add the black pepper and parsley and stir to mix.

Rub the lamb steaks with the olive oil and coat each side with the parsley and spice mixture.

Heat a stove-top grill pan until hot, add the lamb and cook for 2–3 minutes on each side for rare or 4–5 minutes for medium, depending on thickness.

While the lamb is cooking, put the yoghurt, mint and lemon juice in bowl, add salt and pepper to taste and mix well. Carve the steaks into thick slices and serve with the minted yoghurt.

sweet teatime bruschetta

Bruschetta doesn't have to be bread — teacakes can also be toasted on the grill pan. Cook the fruit very briefly, so it just begins to soften and release its sweet juices, without becoming mushy.

2 teacakes, halved

15 g unsalted butter

1 tablespoon caster sugar

**250 g medium strawberries, hulled
   and cut into quarters**

250 g raspberries

clotted or thick cream, to serve

serves 4

Heat a stove-top grill pan until hot. Add the teacake halves and cook for about 1 minute on each side until lightly charred.

Heat the butter in a frying pan until melted. Add the sugar and strawberries and cook for about 1 minute, stirring frequently, until the sugar has dissolved. Add the raspberries and cook for 20–30 seconds. Put a teacake, cut side up, on each serving plate. Spoon over the hot fruit and serve with a dollop of cream.

trout with tarragon and bacon

barbecues

There are many kinds of outdoor barbecues. Some people have electric or gas-fired grills. Others have a kettle-style grill on legs or wheels. For real, smoky barbecue flavour, a wood-fired grill is required, but for nice charred surfaces – though without the woodsmoke scent – grills with special briquettes or charcoal are very accessible.

preparing the barbecue

- Preheat the barbecue to the required temperature. To test, hold the palm of your hand 10 cm from the heat. If you have to pull your hand away in 2 seconds, it's the right heat.

- If using charcoal or wood, never try to cook when there are still flames or the coals are still red – wait until they have a covering of light grey ash.

- If using charcoal or wood, keep the food 5 cm away from the coals for thin cuts, such as kebabs or fish, or up to 15 cm for thick cuts which need to cook for longer.

- Have patience. Allow enough time for the barbecue to reach the right heat. (Then allow enough time for the food to cook properly – food will take longer to cook on a barbecue than by other means.)

barbecue cooking tips

- Cook foods over an even, medium heat. If the temperature is too high, the food will scorch and char on the outside and be raw on the inside.

- Cook beef or lamb at a higher heat than chicken or pork.

- If cooking on skewers, first oil them if they are metal or soak them in water for 30 minutes if they are bamboo.

- Trim excess fat – too much causes the coals to flare up and the food to burn.

- Marinating meat and fish before cooking enhances the flavour and tenderizes the flesh. Shake off the marinade before cooking so the liquid doesn't cause flare-ups.

- Don't prod and prick the food while it's cooking – this will release precious juices, cause flare-ups and cause the food to dry out.

- Use tongs and turn the food only once. Separate tongs should be used for raw and cooked foods.

- If cooking large pieces, start them off in the oven, otherwise the outside will be finished before the middle is cooked.

trout with tarragon and bacon

The bacon keeps the trout moist and stops it breaking up.

8 small trout fillets, skin removed
leaves from a bunch of tarragon
juice of 1 lemon
12 slices rindless bacon, stretched to allow for shrinkage
freshly ground black pepper

to serve
4–5 tablespoons crème fraîche or sour cream
2–3 tablespoons wholegrain mustard
2 lemons, cut into wedges

serves 4

Put 4 of the trout fillets on a board and cover generously with tarragon. Sprinkle with lemon juice and black pepper. Top with the remaining fillets and wrap each pair in 3 slices of bacon to make 4 parcels.

Put the crème fraîche and mustard in a bowl and mix gently. Transfer the trout parcels to a preheated barbecue and cook for about 5 minutes on each side until the bacon is crisp. Serve hot with the crème fraîche and mustard mixture and lemon wedges.

barbecued corn with chilli butter

If you can't find corn with the husks still attached, wrap them in foil before cooking. Other vegetables are also good cooked on the barbecue – try whole peppers (and scrape off the burnt skin before serving), butternut squash or root vegetables like potatoes and carrots (wrapped in foil).

4 ears of corn, with husks

chilli butter
90 g salted butter
2 fresh chillies, deseeded and finely chopped
a bunch of coriander, coarsely chopped
grated zest and juice of 1 lime

serves 4

To make the chilli butter, put the butter, chillies, coriander, lime zest and juice in a bowl and mix.

Put the corn on the preheated barbecue and cook for about 15 minutes, turning occasionally, until charred all over.

To serve, pull back the husks from the corn, spread with a large spoonful of chilli butter and eat at once.

lemon spatchcocked chicken

aubergine steaks with feta salad

seared swordfish with avocado salsa

lemon spatchcocked chicken

Spatchcocked chickens have the backbones removed with scissors and are then opened out flat (buy ready-split or ask the butcher to do it). The chicken cooks through evenly, so is ideal for the barbecue. Cook bony side down first – the bone transfers heat to the flesh.

2 lemons
3 tablespoons olive oil
1 chicken, 1.8 kg, split down the back and opened out flat
a handful of thyme sprigs
freshly ground black pepper

to serve
quick aioli (page 144)
1 lemon, cut into wedges

2 long metal skewers

serves 4

Using a zester, remove the zest from the lemons, leaving behind the white pith (which is very bitter). Cut the lemons in half and squeeze out the juice, reserving the squeezed halves.

Put the oil, lemon zest and juice in a large, shallow dish. Add plenty of black pepper and mix well. Add the split chicken, thyme and squeezed lemon halves, cover and refrigerate for 4–8 hours.

Remove the chicken to a board and discard the marinade. With the wings nearest you, push a skewer through 1 wing diagonally across the chicken and through the opposite leg. Push the second skewer diagonally through the second wing and leg. This will make the chicken easier to turn on the barbecue.

Transfer to the preheated barbecue – bony side down – and cook over medium coals for 20–25 minutes on each side, or until cooked through and lightly charred. Transfer the chicken to a clean wooden board, remove the skewers and serve with Quick Aioli and lemon wedges.

aubergine steaks with feta salad

Barbecues often get a bit meat-heavy, so this is a refreshing change. It's a meal in itself, but it also goes well with lamb.

2 aubergines, about 20 cm, sliced diagonally into 2.5 cm slices
4 tablespoons olive oil
grated zest of 1 lemon
2 tablespoons thyme leaves

feta salad
24 black olives, pitted and coarsely chopped
1 small red onion, diced
½ cucumber, diced
2 tomatoes, about 75 g, diced

75 g feta cheese, crumbled
a bunch of flat leaf parsley, coarsely chopped
3 tablespoons olive oil
1 small garlic clove, crushed
juice of ½ lemon
salt and freshly ground black pepper

serves 4

Put the aubergine slices, oil, lemon zest and thyme in a bowl. Toss to coat and add black pepper to taste. Set aside.

To make the salad, put the olives, onion, cucumber, tomatoes, feta, parsley, oil and garlic in a second bowl and mix gently. Set aside.

Cook the aubergine slices on the preheated barbecue or under a medium grill for about 5 minutes on each side until lightly charred and very soft. Sprinkle the salad with lemon juice, salt and pepper to taste. Divide the aubergine and salad between 4 plates and serve.

seared swordfish with avocado and salsa

Swordfish and tuna are perfect fish for the barbecue – their texture is quite meat-like, so it doesn't flake or fall apart.

2 tablespoons olive oil
grated zest and juice of 2 limes
4 swordfish steaks
2 large, just-ripe avocados, halved, pitted, peeled and sliced
freshly ground black pepper

salsa
1 small red onion, chopped
1 red chilli, deseeded and very finely chopped
1 large ripe tomato, halved, deseeded (page 11) and chopped
3 tablespoons extra virgin olive oil
grated zest and juice of 1 lime

to serve
1 lime, cut into wedges
a bunch of coriander, chopped

serves 4

Put the oil, lime zest and juice into a small bowl and whisk well. Add plenty of black pepper. Put the swordfish steaks in a shallow dish and pour over the oil and lime mixture, making sure the fish is coated on all sides. Cover and refrigerate for up to 1 hour.

Meanwhile, to make the salsa, put the onion, chilli, tomato, oil, lime zest and juice in a bowl. Mix gently, then cover and refrigerate.

Heat the barbecue to hot and cook the fish for about 2–3 minutes on each side or until just cooked through. Divide the avocado slices and fish between 4 plates, spoon over the salsa, sprinkle with coriander and serve with lime wedges.

barbecued steak with sizzled prawns

If you can't find the extra large prawns, use smaller ones, but to make them easier to turn on the barbecue, remove the shell and slide them onto bamboo skewers. Remember to presoak the skewers in water so that they don't catch fire.

12 extra large uncooked, unpeeled prawns

2 tablespoons runny honey

2 tablespoons olive oil

1 garlic clove, sliced

juice of ½ lime or lemon

4 sirloin steaks

2 tablespoons teriyaki sauce

freshly ground black pepper

chunky guacamole (page 143), to serve

serves 4

Put the prawns in a shallow dish. Put the honey, oil, garlic and lime or lemon juice in a bowl and mix well. Pour the mixture over the prawns and sprinkle with pepper. Cover and chill for 30 minutes to marinate.

Put the steaks on a plate and sprinkle with the teriyaki sauce. Transfer the steaks to a high heat on the barbecue and sear for 2–3 minutes on each side for rare, 3–4 minutes for medium and 5–6 minutes for well-done, depending on thickness.

Remove the prawns from their marinade and cook on the hot barbecue for 1–2 minutes on each side, until pink and lightly charred. Brush with the marinade from time to time during cooking.

Put a steak onto each serving plate and put a few prawns on top. Serve with the Chunky Guacamole.

hot boozy berry puddings

These puddings need only a gentle heat to cook, so put them on the barbecue last of all, after the coals have died down. The double foil squares not only give extra strength to avoid punctures, but also stop the bottoms of the muffins from scorching as they heat through.

4 blueberry muffins

125 g blueberries

125 g raspberries

125 ml sweet wine, such as Sauternes or Muscat

250 g mascarpone cheese

grated zest and juice of 1 orange

icing sugar

8 pieces of foil, 25 cm square

serves 4

Cut the muffins in half diagonally from top to bottom. Put the 2 halves of each muffin on a double layered square of foil and scrunch the foil round the base and up the sides of the muffins to keep the 2 halves loosely together and hold them in place, leaving enough room to sandwich berries in the middle.

Divide the blueberries and raspberries between the sliced muffin halves. Pour a quarter of the sweet wine over each muffin and bring the foil together tightly to seal the muffins into a parcel. Cook on the barbecue for about 5–7 minutes, or until steaming hot. Take care when testing or eating them, as the fruit in the middle can get very hot — much hotter than the muffins.

Meanwhile, put the mascarpone in a bowl and beat with a wooden spoon until soft. Add the orange zest and juice and icing sugar to taste. Transfer the parcels to plates, open them up and serve hot, topped with the orange mascarpone.

Cooking meat on the barbecue

• Cook at a high heat first, to seal the outside, then transfer to a cooler part of the grill to cook the inside to your liking.

• Don't cook very thick cuts, or the outside will be overcooked before the inside is done. Make them no more than about 5 cm.

• When cooking pork (and also chicken), make sure it is thoroughly cooked, with no sign of pink in the middle (to check, stick a skewer through the thickest part – the juices should run clear or golden, with no trace of pink).

• Finish cooking in the oven if necessary.

hot boozy berry puddings

grilling

As much as I love the trend these days for grill pans and barbecuing, I try not to let the simple grill at the top of my oven become a forgotten tool. The overhead heat produces a lovely char-grill texture on the outside. It also allows the fat to drain off the food into the tray below, so is a healthy way to cook.

grilling tips

- Preheat the grill to its highest setting until very hot, then adjust the heat according to the recipe. Preheating is essential to seal the outside of meat properly, leaving the middle succulent.

- Tender cuts of meat, such as fillet steaks, lamb cutlets or chicken breast, are best for grilling.

- Use thin cuts, not more than 5 cm thick, for grilling, so that the meat can cook through without the outside burning.

- Don't prod the food with a fork while it is cooking under the grill – you will lose its lovely juices.

- When grilling thick pieces of chicken, or sausages, turn them often with tongs or a spoon and fork, so that they cook through without the surface drying out or burning.

- Keep a constant watch on food as it grills – it is close to the heat and cooks very quickly. If it does cook too fast, lower the grill tray so that it is further from the heat.

- Marinating meat, fish and vegetables before cooking keeps them moist and adds flavour.

- Don't season with salt before grilling, as salt draws out moisture – do it during or after.

venison sausages with port and cranberry ragout

Grilling is the healthy way to cook sausages, with the fat draining away into the grill tray. They are also less likely to split than if you pan-fry them. Turn them often, so that they cook through and brown evenly on the outside. You can make this with any good quality sausages, but the gamey venison goes particularly well with the rich, red sauce.

2 large leeks, cut into 5 mm slices

25 g butter

1 tablespoon plain flour

1 tablespoon sugar

300 ml red wine

3 tablespoons port

150 ml chicken or vegetable stock

a large sprig of rosemary

8 good quality sausages, preferably venison

250 g fresh or frozen cranberries

salt and freshly ground black pepper

mustard mash (page 17), to serve

serves 4

Rinse the leeks well in a bowl of cold water, to remove any grit or dirt, then drain in a sieve. Melt the butter in a large saucepan. Add the leeks and gently fry over medium heat, stirring frequently, for 8–10 minutes until softened and slightly golden.

Preheat the grill to a medium setting.

Add the flour to the saucepan of fried leeks and cook, stirring, for 1 minute. Add the sugar, wine, port, stock, rosemary and plenty of salt and pepper. Bring to the boil, reduce the heat and simmer for about 15–20 minutes.

Meanwhile, put the sausages on the grill tray and cook, turning them frequently, for 15–20 minutes until browned all over and cooked all the way through.

Add the cranberries to the saucepan and simmer for a further 5–6 minutes until they begin to soften and pop. Add salt, pepper and sugar to taste, then serve with the sausages and mustard mash.

charred paprika chicken

Cutting slashes into the surface of the chicken speeds up the grilling time while keeping it moist and tender. The butter mixture runs into the grooves and bastes the chicken.

4 chicken breasts, with skin and bone

50 g butter

4 tablespoons wholegrain mustard

2 teaspoons honey

1 tablespoon sweet paprika

freshly squeezed juice of 1 lemon

salt and freshly ground black pepper

sour cream, to serve

serves 4

Preheat the grill to a medium setting. Using a sharp knife, cut 3 slashes diagonally through the chicken skin and flesh to the bone.

Put the butter, mustard, honey and paprika into a bowl and mix well. Brush the skinless side of the chicken with half the butter mixture and put under the grill for 7–8 minutes. Turn the chicken over, brush with the remaining mixture, and return to the grill for a further 7–8 minutes until cooked through.

Remove the chicken from the grill and sprinkle with the lemon juice. Arrange on a large serving dish and serve with sour cream.

simple grilled peppers

Grilling peppers is one of the best ways to skin them. It also brings out their sweet flavour. Try these squashed onto crusty bread, mixed into freshly cooked pasta, or tossed with rocket and Parmesan shavings as a salad.

1 red pepper, quartered and deseeded

1 orange pepper, quartered and deseeded

1 yellow pepper, quartered and deseeded

4 tablespoons extra virgin olive oil

2 teaspoons balsamic vinegar

1 tablespoon fresh basil leaves

salt and freshly ground black pepper

serves 4

Preheat the grill to a medium setting.

Put the pepper quarters on the grill tray, cut side down. Put under the grill for about 5–8 minutes until the skins are charred and blackened. Remove the peppers to a plastic freezer bag, seal and set aside to cool. The steam inside the bag will loosen the skins and make them easy to scrape off and remove.

Take the cooled peppers out of the bag, then peel and scrape away the charred skin. Discard any juices from the bag.

Put the peppers into a shallow dish. Drizzle with the olive oil and balsamic vinegar. Add salt and pepper to taste and sprinkle with the basil. Cover and set aside at room temperature for 2 hours before serving, for the peppers to soak up the dressing.

whole roasted chicken with prunes and thyme

Roasting is like baking, and cooks the food by indirect heat in a dry enclosed atmosphere, making the outside crisp and the inside tender. Centuries ago, roasting of meat was done in front of an open fire on a turning spit. It's much easier now – all you need is an oven and a roasting tin.

roasting tips

- Always preheat the oven to the correct temperature before adding the food.

- Use a good-quality, heavy-gauge roasting tin.

- Meat and poultry cooks more quickly if it includes the bones. Always follow the recipe and test towards the end of cooking time.

- Some foods, especially chicken or pheasant, can dry out in the oven. Putting streaky bacon over the breast protects the meat and keeps it moist.

- 'Basting' means spooning the pan juices over the food while roasting. Baste or turn the food about every 30 minutes. Don't over-baste or you will lower the oven temperature and the estimated cooking time will be altered. Meat with a good layer of fat needs less basting.

- To brown roasted vegetables evenly, shake or toss them half way through the cooking time.

- Some vegetables – potatoes, fennel, and parsnips – are best par-boiled (page 15) before roasting.

times and temperatures

- Weigh meat and roast using the times given on this page as a guide. However, remember that if the piece of meat is long and thin rather than thick and fat, it will take less time.

- *Chicken and duck:*
  200°C (400°F) Gas 6 for 20 minutes per 500 g, plus 20 minutes.

- *Pork:* without crackling,
  170°C (325°F) Gas 3 for 40 minutes per 500 g.
  If cooking pork with crackling,
  220°C (425°F) Gas 7 for 30 minutes then at 190°C (375°F) Gas 5 for 20 minutes per 500 g.

- *Lamb and beef:* first seal the outside by frying or roasting at the highest possible temperature for 20 minutes. Then cook at 190°C (375°F) Gas 5:
  rare: 15 minutes per 500 g
  medium: 20 minutes per 500 g
  well done: 25 minutes per 500 g

roasting

roast loin of pork with butter-baked apples and cider gravy

When roasting pork with crackling, you start it off in a very hot oven to crackle the skin, then reduce the temperature for the meat to cook more gently.

2.25 kg loin of pork, with skin
olive oil
coarse sea salt

cider gravy
1 tablespoon plain flour
150 ml cider
300 ml chicken stock
salt and freshly ground black pepper

serves 6

Preheat the oven to 220°C (425°F) Gas 7.

Using a large, sharp knife, score the pork skin at ½ cm intervals, cutting through the skin but not right through the fat. This stops the skin from shrinking and turns it into crackling. You can buy pork ready-scored, or ask your butcher to do it for you.

1 Brush the pork skin with oil and sprinkle generously with salt.

2 Rub the oil and salt into the skin.

Transfer to a roasting tin and put in the oven. Roast for 30 minutes, then reduce the oven temperature to 190°C (375°F) Gas 5 and roast for a further 2 hours until the meat is cooked through and the skin has crackled.

3 Transfer the pork to a carving board and cover well with foil. Set aside to rest while you make the gravy.

4 Tip off as much of the fat as possible from the roasting tin, keeping all the meat juices underneath the fat. Put the roasting tin over a high heat, add the flour and stir well to mix.

5 Cook, stirring constantly with a wooden spoon, until the flour has turned brown.

6 Remove from the heat, then add the cider and stock. Stir quickly, then mix with a whisk. Return to the heat and bring to the boil, whisking all the time. Reduce the heat and simmer for 2 minutes. Add salt and pepper to taste and pour into a jug.

7 Uncover the pork and remove the layer of crackling. Carve the flesh into slices and cut the crackling into pieces. Serve hot with Butter-baked Apples (page 82) and the cider gravy.

butter-baked apples

6 large, tart dessert apples
50 g unsalted butter
2 tablespoons finely chopped fresh sage
1 garlic clove, crushed
2 tablespoons Demerara sugar,
    plus extra for sprinkling
150 ml dry cider
freshly ground black pepper

serves 6

1 Using a corer, remove the core of each apple.

2 Score a ring around the middle of each apple with

a sharp knife, to stop the apples bursting as they
cook. Transfer to an ovenproof dish or roasting tin.

3 Put the butter, sage, garlic and sugar in a bowl.

4 Beat with a wooden spoon to mix, adding freshly
ground black pepper to taste.

5 Spoon the sage butter into the cavity of each
apple and sprinkle sugar over the top.

6 Pour the cider into the roasting tin.

7 Put the apples into the oven 35 minutes before
the pork is cooked and bake for 30–35 minutes until
soft all the way through but still keeping their shape.
Serve with the roast pork and cider gravy.

whole roasted chicken with prunes and thyme

To baste the chicken a few times as it cooks, spoon the wine juices over the top. Basting keeps the food moist. To test for doneness, use a small knife or skewer to pierce the fattest part of the leg through to the bone – it is cooked when the juices that run out are clear and there is no trace of pink.

1 chicken, about 1.8 kg
4 red onions, peeled and cut into 6 wedges
250 g ready-to-eat prunes
600 ml red wine
1 teaspoon caster sugar
a bunch of thyme sprigs
25 g butter
salt and freshly ground black pepper

serves 4

Preheat the oven to 200°C (400°F) Gas 6.

Loosely tie the legs of the chicken with string to keep its plump shape while cooking. Sprinkle with salt and pepper and put in a large roasting tin. Put the onions and prunes around the chicken and pour the wine over the top. Sprinkle with the sugar and thyme sprigs. Dot the butter over the chicken, transfer to the preheated oven and roast for about 1½ hours, basting frequently, until the chicken is dark golden brown and the juices run clear.

Remove to a board, carve and serve with the onions and prunes.

roasted potatoes

You can roast potatoes in other oils, such as sunflower, or even in lard, but olive oil is much the healthiest, and delicious with it. The sprinkled flour gives the perfect coating to make the outsides crisp. If you don't have rock salt, which is very coarse and adds an extra crunch, use sea salt.

1 kg potatoes, cut into 5 cm pieces
150 ml olive oil
25 g butter
1 tablespoon plain flour, seasoned with rock salt and freshly
    ground black pepper

serves 4

Preheat the oven to 220°C (425°F) Gas 7.

Put the potatoes into a large saucepan and cover with cold water. Cover with a lid and bring to the boil. Reduce the heat and simmer for 8 minutes to par-boil.

Meanwhile, pour the olive oil into a roasting tin and add the butter. Put into the oven for 5 minutes, until smoking hot.

Drain the potatoes well and return them to the saucepan. Holding the lid on, shake the pan well to roughen the surface of the potatoes. Remove the roasting tin from the oven, add the potatoes and turn them over with a large metal spoon to coat them all over with oil. Sprinkle with the flour, then roast for about 45–50 minutes until crisp and golden. Use a large, metal spoon to push the potatoes around the tin from time to time during cooking, to prevent them from sticking.

orange roasted roots

Roasting butternuts, carrots and sweet potatoes until they caramelize is a fantastic way to bring out their natural sweetness and intense flavours.

1 butternut squash
4 carrots, halved lengthways
8 shallots
2 sweet potatoes, cut into wedges
1 orange, halved crossways
4 tablespoons olive oil
2 large sprigs of rosemary
8 garlic cloves
salt and freshly ground black pepper

serves 4

Preheat the oven to 200°C (400°F) Gas 6. Cut the butternut in half lengthways and peel, using a small, sharp knife. Scoop out the seeds with a metal spoon and discard. Put the cut halves, flat side down, on a board and cut into chunks, about 5 cm.

Put the butternut, carrots, shallots and sweet potatoes into a large roasting tin. Squeeze over the juice from the orange and put the squeezed halves into the tin with the vegetables. Drizzle with the olive oil and put the rosemary on top. Add plenty of salt and black pepper, then transfer to the preheated oven and roast for 20 minutes.

Remove from the oven and add the garlic. Shake the tin and move the vegetables around to stop them sticking. Return them to the oven for a further 20 minutes until tender and slightly caramelized.

Which vegetables are good for roasting?
• *All root vegetables are good roasted – potatoes, carrots, parsnips, beetroot, sweet potatoes and turnips.*
• *Most of the onion family – including onions (whole, halved or in wedges), shallots (eschallots), and garlic. Roast garlic heads whole or separate into (unpeeled) cloves. Guests can peel the cloves before they eat them.*
• *Starchy vegetables like pumpkin and butternut squash.*
• *Squashy ones like peppers, courgettes and aubergines.*
• *Tomatoes – cut them in half and roast them cut side up. I love to serve roasted tomatoes with a few olives added towards the end of roasting time.*

saffron fish roast

Roasted vegetables make a delicious base for grilled fish in this recipe. You can roast rather than grill the fish too, but remember that it will take a very short time, so cook it just until the flesh turns opaque.

2 red onions, cut into wedges
2 red peppers, halved, deseeded and each half cut into 3
500 g new potatoes
1 tablespoon olive oil
250 g baby plum tomatoes
500 g thick, skinless cod fillet, cut into 4 chunks
500 g thick, skinless salmon fillet, cut into 4 slices
½ teaspoon rock or sea salt
1 lemon, cut into wedges, to serve

marinade
a pinch of saffron threads
4 tablespoons finely chopped flat leaf parsley
2 tablespoons extra virgin olive oil
freshly ground black pepper

serves 4

Preheat the oven to 200°C (400°F) Gas 6. Put the saffron in a small bowl, add 3 tablespoons boiling water and set aside to soak.

Put the onions, peppers and potatoes into a large roasting tin. Add the olive oil with salt and pepper to taste and mix well. Transfer to the preheated oven and roast for about 45 minutes, until the vegetables are cooked and slightly charred. Add the tomatoes to the tin and roast for a further 5 minutes.

Meanwhile, to make the marinade, put the saffron and its soaking water into a large bowl, add the remaining marinade ingredients and mix. Put the fish into a shallow dish and pour over the marinade. Cover and refrigerate until needed.

Preheat the grill to medium heat. Remove the fish from its marinade and discard the marinade. Put the fish on top of the vegetables in the roasting tin. Sprinkle with the rock or sea salt and cook under the grill for 10–12 minutes, until the fish is just cooked through.

Divide the fish and vegetables between 4 large serving plates and serve with the lemon wedges.

chicken korma
with almonds and cream

braising

Braising is a variation on poaching. This chapter covers both braising (cooking in just a little liquid) and stewing (cooking in a lot of liquid). The food stews very slowly in an enclosed dish in the oven or on top of the stove, until it becomes very tender, and the sauce and juices rich and flavourful. Curries, stews and spicy tagines are all wonderful examples and very simple to make – once they are in the dish, they more or less look after themselves.

braising tips

- Use a heavy saucepan or flameproof casserole with a well-fitting lid, or a wok for quick braises.

- Trim excess fat from your meat and, if using pieces, make sure they are equally sized so that they cook evenly.

- Many recipes sear the meat and vegetables for a braise before adding the liquid. Searing is done by frying in a pan until all the surfaces are sealed and lightly browned. This produces caramelized flavours and keeps the juices in.

- Don't add too much salt at the beginning, as flavours will become more intense as they cook. You can always add more at the end if necessary.

- Add robust herbs – such as thyme, rosemary and bay leaves – at the beginning of cooking and more delicate herbs – such as coriander, basil and parsley – at the last moment.

- Bring the liquid to the boil first, then immediately reduce the heat to a gentle simmer.

- Keep the temperature constant – braising is a slow method of cooking, so the heat needs to be even and gentle.

- Keep an eye on the level of the liquid in the pan or dish and top it up if necessary – it doesn't have to be stock or wine, often water will do.

reheating

- Braised dishes often taste better if made the day before and reheated. Keep them in the refrigerator overnight and remove any fat from the surface before reheating thoroughly on top of the stove or in the oven.

- Heat them to boiling point first on top of the stove, then transfer to a preheated oven and cook at 160°C (325°F) Gas 3 for about 30 minutes, so the dish is heated right through.

chicken korma with almonds and cream

This mild Indian curry is a typical example of a braise. The spices are fried first to release their aromas, before the other ingredients are added.

3 tablespoons sunflower oil

2 large onions, finely sliced

2 large garlic cloves, crushed

1 tablespoon turmeric

2 teaspoons ground coriander

2 teaspoons ground cumin

10 cardamom pods

1 teaspoon black pepper, cracked

¼ teaspoon freshly grated nutmeg

6 large boneless, skinless, chicken thighs, halved

600 ml chicken stock

juice of 1 lemon

1 bay leaf

150 ml double cream

2 tablespoons ground almonds

2 tablespoons mint, shredded

cooked basmati rice or naan bread, to serve

serves 4

1 Heat 2 tablespoons of the oil in a large, flameproof casserole or wok. Add the onions and fry gently for 15 minutes until softened and beginning to brown.

2 Add the garlic and spices to the onions and fry for about 1 minute. Frying spices releases their aroma. Use your nose to tell how long to fry them — they give a burst of fragrance when they are ready.

3 Heat the remaining oil in a large frying pan and add the chicken pieces.

4 Fry for 2 minutes on each side or until golden, then transfer to the casserole.

5 Add the stock.

6 Add the lemon juice and bay leaf.

7 Bring to the boil.

8 Reduce the heat, cover with a lid and simmer gently for 20–25 minutes until the chicken is cooked through.

9 Add the cream, ground almonds and mint and simmer for a further 2 minutes. Serve hot with basmati rice (page 22) or warmed naan bread.

bean and bacon ragout with rosemary

Canned beans make a hearty, speedy, stove-top braise. Unlike dried beans, they don't need to be soaked and cooked for hours, making this a fast dish to prepare. For vegetarians, omit the bacon and add 125 g sliced fresh shiitake mushrooms at the same time as the onion.

1 tablespoon olive oil

1 large onion, coarsely chopped

125 g thick-cut bacon, cubed

2 garlic cloves, crushed

800 g canned chopped tomatoes

250 g cherry tomatoes

1 tablespoon balsamic vinegar

½ teaspoon sugar

400 g canned cannellini beans, drained and rinsed

400 g canned borlotti beans, drained and rinsed

1 tablespoon chopped fresh rosemary

salt and freshly ground black pepper

to serve

young leaf spinach or rocket

extra virgin olive oil

balsamic vinegar

crusty bread

serves 4

Heat the oil in a large, heavy-based saucepan. Add the onion and cook for 5 minutes until golden.

Add the bacon to the pan and cook, stirring from time to time, for a further 4–5 minutes, until crisp. Add the garlic and cook for another minute. Add the canned and cherry tomatoes, vinegar and sugar. Stir, then bring to the boil. Reduce the heat and simmer for 5 minutes.

Add the cannellini and borlotti beans and the rosemary. Simmer for another 5 minutes until bubbling hot. Add salt and freshly ground black pepper to taste.

Ladle the ragout into 4 large soup plates. Top with a handful of spinach or rocket. Drizzle with olive oil and balsamic vinegar, sprinkle with black pepper and serve with crusty bread.

Browning vegetables

• *Many recipes, especially Western and Indian dishes, brown the vegetables in oil or butter at the beginning of a braise.*

• *This is done to caramelize the natural sugars in the vegetables – it gives more delicious flavour to the dish.*

green thai vegetable curry

This is a super-quick poach-braise – it cooks just long enough for the vegetables to become tender.

3 tablespoons green Thai curry paste

400 ml canned coconut milk

425 ml vegetable stock

1 large potato, cut into 2.5 cm pieces

250 g broccoli florets

250 g cauliflower florets

125 g frozen petit pois

125 g sugar snap peas, halved lengthways

to serve

1 lime, cut into wedges

cooked Thai fragrant rice (page 22)

serves 4

Put the curry paste in a wok, heat and cook for 2 minutes, stirring. Add the coconut milk, stock and potato. Bring to the boil, reduce the heat and simmer for 5 minutes. Add the broccoli and cauliflower florets, stalk end down, cover with a lid and simmer for 4 minutes. Add the peas and sugar snaps and cook for a further 2 minutes until all the vegetables are tender.

Ladle the curry into 4 bowls and serve with lime wedges and Thai fragrant rice.

bean and bacon ragout with rosemary

green thai vegetable curry

beef braised in red wine with light gruyère dumplings

A classic stew – after being seared and browned, the meat cooks very slowly in the oven, giving it time to become beautifully tender and succulent.

20 g dried porcini mushrooms, thoroughly rinsed
2 tablespoons olive oil
1 kg braising beef, cut into 4 cm chunks
425 ml red wine
250 g shallots, peeled and halved lengthways
3 large, open mushrooms, each cut into 8 wedges
1 tablespoon plain flour
1 bay leaf
1 tablespoon thyme leaves

gruyère dumplings
225 g plain flour
¼ teaspoon salt
2½ teaspoons baking powder
55 g Gruyère cheese, grated
3 tablespoons coarsely chopped flat leaf parsley
3 tablespoons chopped chives
2 tablespoons extra virgin olive oil
150 ml milk
salt and freshly ground black pepper

serves 4

Preheat the oven to 150°C (300°F) Gas 2. Put the porcini in a bowl, cover with 600 ml boiling water and leave to soak.

Meanwhile, heat 1 tablespoon of the oil in a large frying pan. Add half the beef and sear on all sides until brown. Using a slotted spoon, remove the beef from the pan and reserve. Repeat with the remaining beef. Add a good splash of the wine to the pan, stir well with a wooden spoon to remove the sediment, then pour into a jug and reserve.

Add the remaining oil to the pan. When hot, add the shallots and fry for 4–5 minutes until golden brown. Add the open mushrooms and fry for a further 4–5 minutes. Sprinkle in the flour and cook, stirring continuously, for 1–2 minutes.

Pour in the remaining wine and reserved beef juices and add the reserved chunks of beef. Add the bay leaf, thyme and porcini with the liquid it has been soaking in. Bring to the boil and transfer to a medium-sized shallow casserole dish. Cover with a lid and cook in the oven for 2 hours.

To make the dumplings, 10 minutes before the 2 hours are up, sift the flour, salt and baking powder into a large bowl. Stir in the Gruyère, 2 tablespoons each of the parsley and chives and plenty of pepper. Add the oil and milk and stir lightly with a fork to form a soft dough.

Transfer the mixture to a floured surface and knead very lightly. Using floured hands, shape into 8 dumplings. Remove the stew from the oven and put the dumplings on top. Return to the oven and cook, uncovered, for 35–40 minutes more, until the dumplings have risen and are golden brown. Sprinkle with the remaining parsley and chives and serve hot.

moroccan lamb tagine

A tagine is a North African stew cooked in a tall, conical pot of the same name. It is traditionally cooked over an open fire, but it also works well cooked in the oven, or in a wok or sauté pan on top of the stove.

1 kg boneless shoulder of lamb, trimmed of about half its fat
    and cut into 5 cm chunks
600 ml chicken stock
2 tablespoons olive oil
1 large onion, coarsely chopped
4 garlic cloves, chopped
1 tablespoon ground cumin
1 tablespoon ground coriander
1 tablespoon hot paprika
400 g canned chopped tomatoes
1 cinnamon stick, broken in half
175 g dried apricots
½ teaspoon freshly ground black pepper
3 large pieces of orange zest

to serve
couscous or cracked wheat (page 141)
50 g pine nuts, lightly toasted (page 11)

orange relish
2 oranges, separated into segments
1 red onion, chopped
1 red chilli, finely chopped (page 43)
leaves from a bunch of coriander
1 tablespoon mint leaves, finely sliced

serves 4

Heat a large, non-stick sauté pan or wok until hot. Add half the lamb chunks and sear on all sides until brown.

Using a slotted spoon, remove the browned lamb from the pan, put it on a plate and set aside. Add about 100 ml of the chicken stock to the sauté pan or wok. Stir with a wooden spoon to remove all the flavourful sediment from the bottom, then pour out into a jug and reserve. Add the remaining lamb to the pan and sear until brown, repeating the chicken stock process.

Return the pan to the heat and add the oil. When hot, add the onion and fry gently for about 10 minutes until golden. Add the garlic and fry for a further 2 minutes. Add the cumin, ground coriander and paprika to the pan and fry for a further minute. Add the reserved browned lamb and the tomatoes, cinnamon, apricots, pepper, orange zest and remaining stock. Bring to the boil and cover with a lid. Reduce the heat and simmer very gently for about 2 hours until the meat is meltingly tender.

Put all the relish ingredients in a bowl and mix.

Serve the tagine sprinkled with pine nuts, accompanied by the relish and couscous or cracked wheat.

Note If cooking in the oven, use an ovenproof casserole dish and follow the recipe up to the point where the dish is covered with a lid. Then transfer to a preheated oven and cook at 150°C (300°F) Gas 2 for about 2 hours, or until the meat is very tender.

moroccan lamb tagine

cherry and cinnamon scones

Cakes and scones, biscuits and cookies, brownies and muffins, breads and pizzas, pies and tarts – it's all baking. They're mostly simple – try the samples in this chapter, then some of those in the chapter beginning on page 146. All you need is an oven and a few basic items of bakeware, listed on page 8.

baking tips

- Weigh and measure all the ingredients before you start to bake. Using accurate amounts is crucial to successful baking.

- Preheat the oven to the correct temperature before putting anything in it. If you're making pizza, preheat the baking sheet or pizza stone as well.

- Bread bakes best at a high heat, so that it rises and develops a nice crust – put it on the top shelf of the oven.

- Cakes are more delicate, so bake them at a lower temperature on the middle shelf of the oven.

- Bread can be made without yeast (page 99). The results are different from yeast-baked breads, but are just as good. Yeast-free bread doesn't keep as long, and is best eaten the day it is made.

- When making open pies, tarts and quiches (page 106) blind-bake the pastry shells. To bake blind means to line a tart tin with pastry, then with paper. Add dried beans or uncooked rice (or special ceramic baking beans) then bake until no longer transparent in a preheated oven at 200°C (400°F) Gas 6. Remove from the oven, remove the paper and beans or rice, then return to the oven for 3–5 minutes to dry out. This will make sure the pastry is cooked and crisp.

- When making pastry, wrap and chill the dough for 20–30 minutes before rolling out. The dough heats up as you are working on it – chilling allows it to cool and rest so it won't shrink too much while cooking.

- Remove baked goods from their tins as soon as they are cooked and put them on a wire rack to cool – that way, no soggy bottoms!

baking

orange and bitter chocolate muffins

Muffins need room to grow – fill the muffin tins only three-quarters full.

280 g plain flour
1½ teaspoons baking powder
1 teaspoon salt
½ teaspoon bicarbonate of soda
225 g caster sugar
100 g plain chocolate (minimum 70 per cent cocoa solids)
1 orange
55 g butter
175 ml milk

12 hole muffin tin, preferably non-stick, lightly buttered

serves 12

Preheat the oven to 190°C (375°F) Gas 5.

1 Sift the flour, baking powder, salt and bicarbonate of soda into a large bowl. Stir in the sugar.

2 Coarsely chop the chocolate.

3 Add the chocolate to the bowl and mix.

4 Make a well in the centre of the dry ingredients.

5 Using the fine setting on a box grater, grate the zest from the orange and set aside. Cut the orange in half crossways. Squeeze the juice from the orange halves.

6 Put the butter into a small saucepan and heat until melted. Pour into a second bowl.

7 Add milk and orange juice to the butter.

8 Pour the butter and orange mixture into the well of the dry ingredients. Stir briefly with a wooden spoon. Don't overmix – it should be lumpy, not smooth.

9 Spoon the mixture into the buttered tin.

Bake in the preheated oven for about 20 minutes until golden and cooked through. (Insert a skewer into the middle of one muffin to test – when it is cooked the skewer will come out clean.)

10 Remove from the oven and let cool for a couple of minutes in the tin.

11 Remove from the tin to a wire rack and serve warm or at room temperature.

Note For cooking, use best-quality cooking chocolate with at least 70 per cent cocoa solids (listed on the wrapper).

Greasing, flouring and lining baking tins

• *'Greasing' means brushing the inside of the tin with a thin film of butter or oil. This stops the food from sticking to the tin when cooked.*

• *Tins are sometimes then dusted with a light layer of flour, or lined with baking parchment on the base, or on the base and sides – also to stop the food sticking.*

• *Lining is usually done if the food is to be baked for a long time – say a large fruit cake.*

black olive pizza crust

Once you have baked the pizza base from the recipe below, you can add whatever you fancy to the cooked crust – try some of the delicious toppings suggested here. They don't need any extra cooking – just top and serve!

225 g strong white flour

3½ g (half a sachet) easy-blend dried yeast

2 tablespoons olive oil, plus extra for drizzling

85 g black olives, pitted and chopped

2 garlic cloves, crushed

3 plum tomatoes, sliced crossways

1 teaspoon caster sugar

a baking sheet or pizza stone, lightly floured

serves 2

Sift the flour into a large bowl and stir in the yeast. Make a well in the centre of the flour, add about 125 ml warm water and the olive oil and mix to make a soft, wet dough.

Transfer the dough to a lightly floured surface. Knead, by pushing the dough away from you with the heel of one hand and holding the end nearest you with the other hand so that it stretches out. Fold the dough back over into a ball shape, give it a quarter turn, and stretch it out again. Repeat this process until it is smooth and elastic, which should take about 10 minutes.

Put the dough in a large, lightly oiled bowl. Cover with clingfilm and leave in a warm place for about 1 hour, or until doubled in size.

Meanwhile, put the baking sheet or pizza stone into the oven and preheat the oven to 230°C (450°F) Gas 8. When the dough has risen,

knock it back by flattening it with your fist. Remove from the bowl to a floured surface. Knead again, gradually incorporating the olives and garlic into the dough as you are kneading.

Divide the dough in 2, and roll out each piece on a floured surface to a circle measuring about 30 cm diameter. Transfer a lightly floured baking tray or pizza stone.

Arrange the tomato slices on top of the pizza. Sprinkle with the sugar, salt and pepper and drizzle generously with olive oil. Bake in the preheated oven for about 15–20 minutes or until the pizza is crisp and the tomatoes have begun to caramelize.

Serve each pizza on a large plate and finish with the chosen topping.

pizza toppings:

rocket, bresaola and parmesan

55 g rocket

8 slices bresaola, torn into pieces

55 g fresh Parmesan cheese shavings (page 11)

extra virgin olive oil

freshly ground black pepper

Top each cooked pizza with the rocket and sprinkle with the bresaola and Parmesan. Sprinkle with oil and black pepper.

mozzarella, pine nuts, capers and basil

175 g mozzarella cheese, preferably buffalo, sliced

55 g pine nuts, toasted (page 11)

4 tablespoons baby capers, drained and rinsed

a large handful of basil leaves, torn
extra virgin olive oil
freshly ground black pepper

Tear the slices of mozzarella over each cooked pizza. Sprinkle with the pine nuts and capers, then top with the basil. Sprinkle with oil and black pepper.

feta, onion, parsley and lemon

200 g feta cheese, crumbled into large chunks
½ red onion, finely chopped
a large handful of flat leaf parsley, about 25 g
2 tablespoons extra virgin olive oil
1 tablespoon lemon juice

Put all the ingredients in a bowl and mix well. Divide the mixture between the 2 cooked pizzas and serve immediately.

gorgonzola and walnut bread with crunchy celery salad

An easy, yeast-free bread for a beginner baker. For real indulgence, serve with an extra slab of Gorgonzola.

225 g wholemeal flour
225 g plain flour
1 teaspoon bicarbonate of soda
2 teaspoons cream of tartar
1 teaspoon salt
1 teaspoon caster sugar
½ teaspoon cracked black pepper
25 g butter, melted

300 ml milk
175 g Gorgonzola cheese, roughly crumbled
85 g walnut pieces, lightly toasted (page 11)

celery salad
6 celery stalks, sliced diagonally
1 small red onion, finely chopped
2 tart dessert apples, cored and coarsely chopped
freshly squeezed juice of 1 lemon
2 tablespoons extra virgin olive oil
75 g watercress, washed
freshly ground black pepper

a baking sheet, floured

serves 4

Preheat the oven to 190°C (375°F) Gas 5.

Sift the dry ingredients into a large bowl. Put the melted butter and milk into a second bowl and mix.

Make a large well in the centre of the dry ingredients, pour in the butter and milk mixture and, using a wooden spoon, mix to a soft dough. Add the Gorgonzola and walnuts to the dough and knead gently.

Turn out onto a floured surface and shape into a rough oval about 5 cm thick. Transfer to a floured baking sheet and, using a sharp knife, make 3 diagonal slashes across the surface of the bread. Dust with a little extra flour and bake in the preheated oven for about 40 minutes until cooked and golden with an evenly crisp base. Transfer to a wire rack and let cool for 20 minutes.

Meanwhile, put the salad ingredients into a large bowl and toss gently. Add black pepper to taste and transfer to a serving bowl. Cut the bread into thick chunks, transfer to a wooden board and serve with the salad.

cherry and cinnamon scones

For light scones that are nicely risen, handle the dough gently and as little as possible. The mixture needs plenty of air, which is why you sift the dry ingredients.

280 g plain flour
1 tablespoon baking powder
½ teaspoon salt
1 teaspoon ground cinnamon
55 g unsalted butter, diced
25 g caster sugar
150 ml milk
1 egg, beaten
175 g canned black cherries, drained and coarsely chopped

a baking sheet, floured

serves 6

Preheat the oven to 220°C (425°F) Gas 7.

Sift the flour, baking powder, salt and cinnamon into a large bowl and mix. Stir in the diced butter, then using the tips of your fingers, rub in the butter lightly until the mixture looks like coarse breadcrumbs. Add the sugar and stir to mix.

Put the milk and egg into a second bowl and mix. Make a well in the centre of the dry ingredients and pour the milk and egg mixture into the well. Stir in the cherries and, using a round bladed or palette knife, gently bring the mixture together to form a soft dough.

Turn out onto a floured surface and knead very briefly for 30 seconds until just smooth. Do not over-knead or the scones will be tough.

Using your hands, press out to a rough circle, about 2.5 cm thick. Cut into 6 wedges and transfer to the floured baking sheet.

Dust lightly with flour and bake for 18–20 minutes until risen and golden. Eat hot, or let cool on a wire rack.

crusted lime polenta cake

Fill the cake tin only three-quarters full – the cake will expand as it cooks. Cakes need to cook for longer than scones in a low, gentle oven heat.

225 g unsalted butter
225 g caster sugar
3 eggs, beaten
½ teaspoon vanilla essence
225 g ground almonds
grated zest and juice of 3 limes
115 g polenta flour
1 teaspoon baking powder
a pinch of salt

lime crust
juice of 2 limes
3 tablespoons caster sugar
mascarpone or coconut and lime ice cream (page 150), to serve

a loose-based cake tin, 25 cm diameter, buttered and floured

serves 8–10

Preheat the oven to 160°C (325°F) Gas 3. Put the butter and sugar into a large mixing bowl and beat with an electric whisk until pale and light. Gradually add the eggs, whisking all the time. Using a large metal spoon, stir in the vanilla essence and ground almonds, then fold in the lime zest and juice, polenta flour, baking powder and salt.

Spoon into the prepared cake tin and bake for about 1 hour 15 minutes or until just set and golden brown.

Meanwhile, to make the lime crust, put the lime juice and sugar into a bowl and mix well.

When the cake is cooked, prick well with a skewer all over the surface and pour over the lime crust mix. Let cool for 15 minutes in the tin.

Remove from the tin and serve still warm or let cool completely before slicing. Serve with mascarpone or coconut ice cream.

Tips on buying bakeware
• I buy only non-stick bakeware, because it's very user-friendly.
• Treat non-stick bakeware gently – don't scrub or scrape it.
• Buy the best you can afford – the food won't stick to it, and it won't go rusty.

crusted lime polenta cake

the recipes

Now you know the basics, it's time to make use of your new-found skills. Enjoy these fabulous recipes, impress your friends and discover how simple it all is. Don't be afraid of making mistakes – it's all part of the process.

rocket eggs with salsa verde

rocket eggs
with salsa verde

An omelette-style dish which is fast to cook – have the ingredients ready before you start. To serve more than two people, double the ingredients, but make the eggs in two batches.

4 organic or free range eggs

1 teaspoon unsalted butter

50 g wild rocket

salt and freshly ground black pepper

to serve

125 g mixed salad leaves

25 g walnuts, broken into pieces

**fresh Parmesan cheese shavings
  (page 11)**

1 recipe rocket salsa verde (page 143)

serves 2

Crack the eggs into a small bowl and whisk briefly to break up. Add salt and pepper to taste.

Heat the butter in a wok or frying pan until foaming. Add the rocket and cook, stirring, for about 30 seconds.

Add the eggs and gently swirl around the surface of the wok. Cook until golden brown underneath, but still slightly soft and runny on the top.

Meanwhile, divide the salad between 2 plates and sprinkle with the walnuts. Using 2 wooden spoons, cut the omelette into 4 pieces and put on top of the salad. Top with Parmesan shavings and serve at once with the salsa verde.

quails' eggs
with three salts

These are really just tiny hard-boiled eggs, but more fun and unusual than hens' eggs. If you use hens' eggs, increase the cooking time to 6 minutes.

16 quails' eggs

2 teaspoons celery salt

chilli salt

1 teaspoon salt

1 teaspoon chilli powder

black pepper salt

1 teaspoon coarse sea salt

1 teaspoon freshly ground black pepper

serves 4

Put the eggs in a saucepan, cover with cold water and bring to the boil. Reduce the heat and simmer for 3 minutes.

Drain and tip the eggs into a bowl of cold water to stop them cooking any further. Let cool in the water, then drain and peel.

To serve, put the quails' eggs in a bowl and the salts in individual small pots. Hand round the eggs and dip into the salt of your choice.

A carton of eggs is the one thing I always have in my fridge. Not only are they the ultimate in fast food, they are also very versatile – eat them hot or cold, on their own, or combined with other foods to make all sorts of sweet or savoury dishes.

smoked salmon and dill quiche

The secret to good pastry is to have all the ingredients as cold as possible. Baking the pastry case (baking blind) before adding the filling ensures a crisp base. If you don't have a food processor or don't want to make your own pastry, you can buy ready-to-roll fresh or frozen shortcrust pastry in supermarkets. If frozen, thaw before rolling out.

pastry

280 g plain flour

a pinch of salt

140 g chilled butter, diced

2 egg yolks

2 tablespoons very cold water

filling

leaves from a bunch of dill, coarsely chopped

2 tablespoons olive oil

1 tablespoon Dijon mustard

325 ml crème fraîche

2 whole eggs, plus 2 egg yolks (below, right)*

175 g smoked salmon

salt and freshly ground black pepper

a loose-based tart tin, 25 cm diameter
greaseproof paper and baking beans or uncooked rice

serves 8

Put all the pastry ingredients into a food processor and blend until the ingredients just come together. Don't process beyond this point or the pastry will be tough. Bring the mixture together with your hands and pat into a disc the size of a large plate. Wrap in clingfilm and refrigerate for 20 minutes. This lets the pastry relax, making it easier to roll out and line the tart tin. It also prevents the pastry shrinking too much during cooking.

Preheat the oven to 200°C (400°F) Gas 6. Put the pastry on a lightly floured surface and roll out a disc to just bigger than the tart tin. Roll the pastry around the rolling pin and drape it over the tart tin. Carefully press the pastry into the tin, making sure there are no air pockets. Cut off excess pastry from the edges. Refrigerate for 15 minutes.

Put the dill, olive oil and mustard in a mini-blender. Process until the mixture comes together, then add salt and pepper.

Line the pastry case with greaseproof paper and fill with baking beans or uncooked rice. (This stops the pastry from shrinking and puffing up.) Bake in the preheated oven for 10–15 minutes, then remove the greaseproof paper and beans and return the tart case to the oven for a further 3–5 minutes until just cooked.

Reduce the oven temperature to 180°C (350°F) Gas 4 while you prepare the filling.

Put the crème fraîche in a bowl, add the whole eggs and yolks and beat with a wooden spoon. Add salt and pepper to taste. Spoon the mustard-dill mixture over the base of the tart case. Arrange the smoked salmon on top, then pour in the egg mixture. Bake in the preheated oven for 30–35 minutes until just set. Serve hot, warm or cold.

courgette quiche with sun-dried tomatoes

Follow the pastry recipe for Smoked Salmon and Dill Quiche (left) for this recipe too. When you have made the pastry case, you can try out different fillings, for instance sun-dried peppers in place of the sun-dried tomatoes.

1 prepared baked pastry case (left)

2 tablespoons olive oil

750 g courgettes, sliced diagonally

325 ml crème fraîche

2 whole eggs, plus 2 egg yolks (below)*

5–6 pieces sun-dried tomatoes in olive oil,
drained and coarsely chopped

salt and freshly ground black pepper

serves 8

Preheat the oven to 200°C (400°F) Gas 6 and make the pastry as in the previous recipe, so that you have a cooked pastry case ready for the filling.

While the pastry is baking blind, put a few drops of the oil into a frying pan and wipe it over the surface with kitchen paper. Heat until hot, add the courgettes and fry in batches until golden on both sides.

Reduce the oven temperature to 180°C (350°F) Gas 4 while you prepare the filling.

Put the crème fraîche in a bowl, add the whole eggs and yolks and beat with a wooden spoon. Add salt and pepper to taste. Arrange the courgette slices in the cooked pastry case, sprinkle with the sun-dried tomatoes, then pour in the egg mixture.

Bake in the preheated oven for about 30–35 minutes until golden and set. Serve hot, warm or cold.

*Don't waste the extra egg whites. Freeze them, then use to make Pavlova (page 146). Defrost completely before beating.

courgette quiche with sun-dried tomatoes

french toast with smoky bacon and spiked tomatoes

Day-old bread is best for this recipe as it will soak up more of the eggy mixture and fry better than fresh bread. The eggs make the bread puff up inside like a delicious soufflé.

4 eggs

4 slices thick white bread, halved diagonally

12 slices smoked streaky bacon

2 tablespoons olive oil

4 large plum tomatoes, halved lengthways

2 teaspoons sugar

2 teaspoons chilli oil

25 g butter

2 tablespoons basil leaves, torn

salt and freshly ground black pepper

serves 4

Preheat the grill. Put the eggs in a bowl and whisk until mixed. Add plenty of salt and pepper. Pour into a large, shallow dish, then dip the slices of bread in the egg mixture, coating it all over, and set aside for a few minutes to let the egg soak into the bread.

Meanwhile, grill the bacon for 1–2 minutes on each side until crisp. Transfer to a low oven to keep it warm.

Heat 1 tablespoon of the olive oil in a frying pan until hot. Add the tomatoes and sprinkle with the sugar. Fry for 1–2 minutes on each side until caramelized. Sprinkle with the chilli oil and remove from the heat. Transfer to a plate and put into a very low oven to keep warm.

Wipe the frying pan clean with kitchen paper, add the butter and remaining oil and heat until hot. Add the egg-soaked bread, in 2 batches if necessary, and fry for 2 minutes on each side until crisp and golden.

Cut the slices of French toast in half diagonally and put 2 triangles on each plate with 3 pieces of bacon on top. Spoon the tomatoes over the bacon, sprinkle with the basil and serve immediately.

parmesan and gruyère soufflés with hot tomato and basil chutney

Don't be afraid of soufflés! They are surprisingly easy to make, and these are part-baked in advance, which takes any timing stresses away. They make great use of eggs – the yolks to set the mixture and whisked whites to give them their light, airy quality. Make sure that everyone is sitting down ready to eat when the soufflés come out of the oven – you have to serve them straight away.

300 ml milk
1 slice of onion
a pinch of freshly grated nutmeg
1 bay leaf
45 g butter
45 g plain flour
1 teaspoon wholegrain mustard
50 g Gruyère cheese, grated
50 g Parmesan cheese, freshly grated
3 large eggs, separated (page 110)
200 ml double cream
salt and freshly ground black pepper
a handful of rocket leaves, to serve

hot tomato and basil chutney
1 tablespoon extra virgin olive oil
1 large shallot, finely chopped
250 g baby plum tomatoes, halved
a pinch of brown sugar
2 tablespoons balsamic vinegar
a squeeze of fresh lemon juice
2 tablespoons torn basil leaves
salt and freshly ground black pepper

6 ramekins, 150 ml each, well buttered

serves 6

To make the chutney, heat the oil in a saucepan. Add the shallot and cook over medium heat for 2–3 minutes. Add the tomatoes, sugar and vinegar and cook for 5–6 minutes, until the tomatoes just begin to soften. Add the lemon juice and plenty of salt and pepper. Stir in the basil.

Put the milk, onion, nutmeg and bay leaf into a saucepan and heat gently until just boiling. Remove the pan from the heat and set aside to infuse for 30 minutes. Remove and discard the onion and bay leaf. Preheat the oven to 180°C (350°F) Gas 4.

Melt the butter in a second saucepan. Add the flour and cook gently, stirring, for 30 seconds. Remove the pan from the heat and gradually add the milk, whisking all the time, until you have a smooth sauce. Return the pan to the heat and stir until the sauce boils and thickens.

Remove the pan from the heat and stir in the mustard, three-quarters of the Gruyère and Parmesan, then the egg yolks. Add salt and pepper to taste.

Put the egg whites in a large, clean bowl and whisk with a metal whisk until stiff. Using a large metal spoon, carefully fold the whites into the cheese mixture until no flecks of white are showing. Pour into the ramekins to two-thirds full.

Put the ramekins in a roasting tin and pour boiling water into the tin to come halfway up the ramekins. This provides a gentle, even heat which stops the eggs separating as they cook. Bake in the preheated oven for 15–20 minutes until set. Remove the ramekins from the tin and set aside to cool.

Before serving, preheat the oven to 220°C (425°F) Gas 7. Loosen the soufflé edges with a knife and turn them out into a shallow ovenproof dish. Sprinkle with the remaining Gruyère and Parmesan and pour over the cream.

Transfer to the oven for about 10–12 minutes, until puffed and golden. Serve at once with a few rocket leaves and a spoonful of hot tomato and basil chutney.

salami and thyme popovers

Egg-based batters can be made savoury or sweet. These popovers are savoury, the clafoutis and frittata (right) are both sweet. The popovers are an updated version of the British classic, toad-in-the-hole – the egg yolks add richness to the batter, while the whites make the cooked popovers light and puffy. Serve them as an accompaniment to other dishes, such as roasted meats or other main courses, or the other dishes listed below. You can also serve them as a starter, with a crisp salad and tomato chutney.

115 g plain flour
a good pinch of salt
2 eggs
300 ml milk
8 teaspoons olive oil
4 tablespoons thyme leaves
115 g salami, skinned and chopped into 1 cm cubes
freshly ground black pepper

12-hole muffin tin

serves 4

Preheat the oven to 220°C (425°F) Gas 7.

Sift the flour and salt into a large bowl. Make a well in the centre and crack the eggs into the well. Using a wooden spoon, gradually mix the eggs into the flour. Using a metal whisk, slowly whisk in the milk, until you have a smooth batter. Cover and refrigerate for 30 minutes.

Put 1 teaspoon olive oil into 8 of the muffin holes and put in the hot oven until smoking hot. Add plenty of freshly ground black pepper to the batter and stir in the thyme. Pour the batter into the 8 hot muffin holes and sprinkle with the salami. Return them to the oven for about 20–25 minutes until risen and golden.

Serve either with Bean and Bacon Ragout with Rosemary (page 90) or spinach and green bean salad (page 126).

plum clafoutis

These baby versions of the popular French pudding are made with sweet egg batter. Clafoutis is usually made with cherries, which you can also use in this recipe in place of plums – apricots, nectarines, blueberries or blackcurrants are good substitutes too. If you have any leftover batter, refrigerate for up to one day and use for pancakes.

115 g plain flour
a good pinch of salt
55 g caster sugar
2 eggs
300 ml milk
1 teaspoon vanilla essence
8 teaspoons sunflower oil
4 plums, halved and pitted

to serve
icing sugar
extra thick double cream

12-hole muffin tin

makes 8

Preheat the oven to 220°C (425°F) Gas 7.

Sift the flour and salt into a large bowl and stir in the sugar. Make a well in the centre and crack the eggs into the well. Using a wooden spoon, gradually mix the eggs into the flour. Using a metal whisk, slowly whisk in the milk, until you have a smooth batter. Stir in the vanilla essence. Cover and refrigerate for 30 minutes.

Put 1 teaspoon sunflower oil into 8 of the holes in the muffin tin and put into the preheated oven until smoking hot. Pour the batter into the 8 muffin holes until half full, then put one plum half, skin side up, in each hole.

Return them to the oven for 20–25 minutes until risen and golden. Dust with icing sugar and serve with cream.

Separating eggs

Have 2 bowls ready. Tap the egg on the side of one bowl to crack it in the middle. Using your thumbs, pull open the two halves with the cracked side facing upwards, tipping the yolk into one half and letting any white fall into the bowl. Tip the yolk back and forth between the 2 shell halves until there is no white left around the yolk. Tip the yolk into the other bowl. If any yolk slips into the white, use a shell to scoop it out.

sweet blueberry and cinnamon frittata with maple syrup

This dish is a cross between a soufflé and an omelette – two of the great egg dishes. It starts on top of the stove like an omelette and is finished in the oven like a soufflé. Make sure you use a pan with an ovenproof handle so it's suitable for both. You need good quality (and therefore more expensive) maple syrup for this recipe.

4 eggs, separated (below, left)

2 teaspoons ground cinnamon

50 g caster sugar

150 g mascarpone cheese

25 g unsalted butter

250 g blueberries

to serve

vanilla ice cream

3 tablespoons good quality maple syrup

non-stick ovenproof frying pan, 30 cm diameter

serves 6

Preheat the oven to 190°C (380°F) Gas 5. Put the egg yolks, the cinnamon and half the sugar into a large bowl. Using an electric whisk, beat the mixture until pale and creamy. Add the mascarpone and whisk for a further minute until smooth.

Remove the beaters from the whisk and wash and dry them. Put the egg whites into a large, clean bowl and whisk until stiff. Add the remaining sugar and beat for a further 2 minutes until stiff and shiny.

Using a large metal spoon, fold 1 spoonful of the egg whites into the egg and mascarpone mixture. Gently fold in the remaining egg whites.

Heat the butter in the frying pan until foaming. Add the egg mixture and cook over a medium heat for 1 minute.

Dot the blueberries over the top, transfer to the preheated oven and bake for about 25 minutes until golden and just set. Serve with ice cream and maple syrup.

tomato tapenade salad

salads

This chapter is called salads, but salads aren't just lettuce. You can make them with lots of other things and serve them at any time of day – even as a meal on their own.

tomato tapenade salad

In Provence, a tapenade is a paste of anchovies, capers and olives, but I've used just capers and olives as the basis for the salad. Use the ripest red tomatoes, so there are plenty of lovely juices to soak up with the toasted focaccia.

1 small focaccia bread, torn into bite-sized pieces

8 large tomatoes, each chopped into 8 pieces

20 kalamata olives, squashed and pitted

2 tablespoons baby capers, rinsed and drained

1 garlic clove, chopped

2 tablespoons extra virgin olive oil

½ teaspoon salt

a pinch of sugar

freshly ground black pepper

to serve

a bunch of basil leaves, torn

extra virgin olive oil

a baking sheet

serves 4

Preheat the oven to 220°C (425°F) Gas 7. Put the focaccia pieces onto a baking sheet. Put in the preheated oven and bake for 12–15 minutes until golden.

Meanwhile, put the tomatoes into a large bowl. Add the olives, capers, garlic, oil, salt, sugar and black pepper.

Divide the toasted focaccia pieces between 4 large serving plates and top with a large spoonful of the tomato mixture. Sprinkle with basil and oil, then serve.

hot crunchy croutons with smoked bacon and avocado

One of my all-time favourite warm salads. Don't slice the avocado until the last minute, so that it doesn't discolour – you can do this while the croutons are cooking in the oven.

125 g pancetta or bacon, cut into 2 cm pieces

1 tablespoon olive oil

3 thick slices rustic-style bread, cut into bite-sized pieces

1 cos lettuce, washed, dried and torn into large pieces

1 butterhead lettuce, washed, dried and torn into large pieces

1 recipe Dijon Dressing (page 145)

2 ripe Hass avocados, halved, pitted, peeled and thickly sliced diagonally

freshly ground black pepper

a large, non-stick baking sheet

serves 4

Preheat the oven to 200°C (400°F) Gas 6. Put the pancetta or bacon on the baking sheet, put into the oven and bake for 5 minutes.

Add the oil and bread and turn it with a spoon to coat the bread. Sprinkle with pepper. Return to the oven and bake for a further 20–25 minutes, moving the bread around the tray with a large spoon a few times during cooking to stop it sticking, until the bread is golden and the bacon is crisp.

Put the lettuce into a large salad bowl, add the dressing and toss gently. Put the avocado, hot bacon and croutons over the salad, toss again and serve immediately.

seared peppered beef salad with horseradish dressing

A summery way of enjoying roast beef without too much heat from the kitchen. Par-boiling the potatoes before roasting means that they won't dry out and shrivel as they roast (see Roasting on page 79 for cooking tips).

500 g baby new potatoes, unpeeled, par-boiled for
   12–15 minutes (page 15), until nearly cooked through
2 tablespoons olive oil
250 g baby plum tomatoes
4 fillet steaks, 125 g each
1 tablespoon Worcestershire sauce
100 g wild rocket
125 g sugar snap peas, trimmed, blanched, refreshed
   (page 15) and halved lengthways
salt and freshly ground black pepper

horseradish dressing
3 tablespoons crème fraîche
1–2 tablespoons creamed horseradish
a squeeze of fresh lemon juice

serves 4

Preheat the oven to 220°C (425°F) Gas 7.

Put the par-boiled potatoes in a roasting tin and toss with 1 tablespoon oil, to coat. Sprinkle with salt and black pepper, transfer to the preheated oven and roast for 25–30 minutes until browned and starting to crisp.

Remove from the oven and, using a large metal spoon, push the potatoes to one end of the tin, in a pile. Put the baby plum tomatoes into the empty half of the tin and sprinkle with 1 tablespoon olive oil, salt and pepper. Roast in the oven for 15 minutes until just soft.

Meanwhile, put all the dressing ingredients into a bowl and mix. Add salt and pepper to taste.

Sprinkle the steaks with plenty of black pepper and drizzle with the Worcestershire sauce. Preheat a stove-top grill pan, add the beef and sear for 1–2 minutes on each side or until cooked to your liking. Set aside to rest.

Put the rocket and the sugar snap peas into a bowl and toss well. Divide between 4 serving plates. Spoon the potatoes and tomatoes around the rocket and peas.

Slice the beef fillet diagonally and arrange the slices over the salad. Top with a dollop of horseradish dressing and serve, with any remaining sauce served separately.

peppered goats' cheese

Cheese, especially blue, goats' milk or creamy, make easy, excellent salads. Gentle cooking gives this one extra pizzazz (you need cheese with a rind if you're going to cook it). Serve it as a starter or for lunch.

1 tablespoon freshly ground black pepper
2 goats' cheeses, 100 g each, with rind, halved crossways
2 large handfuls of wild rocket
2 large handfuls of baby leaf spinach
1 tablespoon extra virgin olive oil
juice of ½ lemon
salt
chilli oil, to serve (optional)

serves 4

Sprinkle the pepper onto a plate and lightly press both sides of each cheese half into the pepper to coat.

Heat a stove-top grill pan until hot. Add the peppered cheese slices, cut side down, and cook for 2 minutes. Turn them over, cover loosely with foil and cook for a further 4–5 minutes until the cheese is soft but not melted.

Meanwhile, put the rocket, spinach, oil and lemon juice into a large bowl. Add salt to taste and toss to coat.

Divide the salad between 4 large serving plates or flat bowls and top with a slice of peppered cheese. Sprinkle with chilli oil, if using, and serve.

seared peppered beef salad
with horseradish dressing

endive, chicory and radicchio
salad with walnut dressing

endive, chicory and radicchio salad with walnut dressing

The secret of this salad is to have the walnuts sizzling hot. Get the salad ready and add the walnuts as soon as they come out of the oven. Walnut oil is great in dressings, but just use extra olive oil if you can't find it. Keep nuts and nut oils (except peanut oil) in the refrigerator, because they can go rancid quickly.

100 g walnuts
1 teaspoon walnut oil
1 teaspoon salt
1 head of radicchio, leaves separated, washed and dried
2 heads of chicory, leaves separated, washed and dried
1 small curly endive lettuce, leaves separated,
    washed and dried

walnut dressing
1 tablespoon walnut oil
1 tablespoon extra virgin olive oil
a good squeeze of fresh lemon juice
freshly ground black pepper

serves 4

Preheat the oven to 200°C (400°F) Gas 6.

Put the walnuts, walnut oil and salt in a small bowl and stir. Transfer to a baking sheet in a single layer and cook in the oven for 8–10 minutes until toasted all over.

Meanwhile, put the salad leaves into a large salad bowl. Put all the dressing ingredients into a separate bowl and whisk well. Add freshly ground black pepper to taste.

To serve, sprinkle the hot walnuts over the salad leaves, pour over the dressing and toss well. Serve immediately as a salad or with crusty bread and shavings of Parmesan (page 11) as a lunch or salad starter.

Washing and drying salad leaves
• *Wash crisp-leafed lettuces and other salad leaves in a bowl of water, transfer to a salad spinner and spin dry. Wrap, put in a cloth or kitchen paper and store in the refrigerator – the leaves will become even crisper.*
• *Rinse soft-leafed greens such as lamb's lettuce or rocket just before using and let drain in a colander. Pat dry with kitchen paper and serve as soon as possible.*
• *If you haven't got a salad spinner, wash the leaves, then pat dry with kitchen paper.*

tuna carpaccio salad

Carpaccio is usually raw beef, but this recipe uses lightly seared tuna instead. As it will be served very rare, make sure the tuna you buy is really fresh – and remember that it carries on cooking after you take it out of the pan.

3 tablespoons teriyaki sauce
1 teaspoon runny honey
juice of 2 limes
4 tablespoons peanut oil
2 very fresh thick tuna steaks
freshly ground black pepper

salad
175 g beansprouts
6 radishes, thinly sliced
1 tablespoon toasted sesame seeds (page 11)
a large bunch of coriander
2.5 cm piece of fresh ginger, peeled and finely chopped
salt and freshly ground black pepper
1 lime, cut into wedges, to serve

serves 4

To make the marinade, put the teriyaki sauce, honey, lime juice and 1 tablespoon peanut oil in a bowl and whisk well. Add black pepper to taste. Remove 3 tablespoons of the marinade and reserve. Add the tuna to the remaining marinade, cover and refrigerate for up to 2 hours.

When ready to serve, put the beansprouts, radishes, sesame seeds and coriander in a large bowl and toss gently. Add plenty of salt and black pepper. Put the ginger, reserved marinade and remaining oil in a bowl. Whisk well.

Heat a large, dry frying pan until very hot. Add the tuna, sear for 1 minute on each side, then remove from the pan to a chopping board. Let rest for 2 minutes and, using a very sharp knife, cut the tuna into thin slices, about 1 cm thick. Divide the slices between 4 serving plates, covering the whole surface of the plate in a single, overlapping layer.

Put a handful of the beansprout salad in the centre of each plate and drizzle with the dressing. Serve with the lime wedges.

wild mushroom soup with sour cream and chives

Dried porcini have a gorgeous, intense taste and you only need to add a few to fresh mushrooms to produce a lovely, rich soup. Always rinse porcini well, to remove dust or grit.

10 g dried porcini mushrooms, rinsed thoroughly
50 g butter
500 g large open mushrooms, sliced
2 garlic cloves, crushed
50 g white bread, crusts removed
150 ml sour cream
a small bunch of chives, chopped
salt and freshly ground black pepper

serves 4

Put the porcini in a small bowl. Cover with 750 ml boiling water and let soak for 30 minutes.

Meanwhile, put the butter into a large saucepan or non-stick wok and heat until melted. Add the sliced mushrooms and cook for about 5 minutes until soft.

Drain the porcini, reserving the soaking liquid. Coarsely chop, then add to the mushrooms in the pan. Cook for a further 2 minutes, then add the garlic.

Tear the bread into the pan. Add the reserved porcini soaking liquid and salt and pepper to taste. Bring to the boil, reduce the heat and simmer for 10 minutes.

Transfer the soup to a food processor or blender and process until almost smooth. Ladle into bowls and top with a spoonful of sour cream. Sprinkle with chives and freshly ground black pepper, then serve.

green minestrone

Moving away from the traditional tomato and meat flavour, this vibrant soup is spring and summer in a bowl.

2 tablespoons olive oil
2 leeks, washed and finely sliced
150 ml white wine
1.5 litres vegetable stock
125 g spaghetti, broken into 5 cm pieces
125 g baby asparagus, halved
125 g fine green beans, trimmed and halved
125 g frozen peas, preferably petit pois
2 courgettes, trimmed and cut into ½ cm dice
leaves from a large bunch of basil, torn
salt and freshly ground black pepper

to serve
fresh Parmesan cheese shavings (page 11)
extra virgin olive oil

serves 4

Heat the oil in a large saucepan or non-stick wok. Add the leeks and fry gently for about 10 minutes, until softened but not golden. Pour in the wine and stock, add salt and pepper to taste and bring to the boil. Add the spaghetti and simmer for 8 minutes.

Add the asparagus and beans and cook for 1 minute. Add the peas and courgettes, return to the boil and simmer for 2 minutes. Add the basil and salt and pepper to taste.

Ladle the minestrone into 4 deep plates or bowls. Sprinkle with the Parmesan shavings and oil. Add plenty of freshly ground black pepper and serve.

I'm a big fan of one-pot meals, so I love soups. Smooth and elegant or chunky and hearty – homemade soup is hard to beat and is incredibly quick to make.

soups

miso chicken broth
with noodles

miso chicken broth with noodles

Furikake is a Japanese seasoning made from sesame seeds and dried seaweed. You can buy it in most big supermarkets, but if you can't find it, use toasted sesame seeds instead.

300 g boneless, skinless chicken breast, thinly sliced

2 tablespoons shoyu (Japanese soy sauce) or soy sauce

2.5 cm piece of fresh ginger, peeled and finely chopped

400 g dried udon or egg noodles

125 g baby leaf spinach

2 spring onions, finely sliced diagonally

4 teaspoons furikake seasoning

chicken broth

900 ml fresh chicken stock

1 sachet instant miso soup

4 tablespoons shoyu or soy sauce

2 garlic cloves, sliced

1 teaspoon sugar

125 g shiitake mushrooms, stalks removed and discarded, caps thickly sliced

serves 4

Put all the broth ingredients into a saucepan. Add 300 ml cold water and bring to the boil. Reduce the heat and simmer for 15–20 minutes.

Put the chicken, shoyu and ginger in a bowl and set aside to marinate.

Cook the noodles in a saucepan of boiling water for 10–12 minutes for udon or 4–5 minutes for egg noodles, until tender, or follow the instructions on the packet. Drain.

Add the chicken and its marinade to the broth and simmer gently for 1–2 minutes. Add the spinach and simmer for a further 1 minute.

Divide the noodles between 4 deep bowls and pour the broth over the top.

Sprinkle with the spring onions and furikake seasoning and serve at once.

watercress and bacon chowder

Chowder is a hearty soup, originally from New England and often made with seafood, especially clams. This version is seafood-free, but has all the robust goodness of a classic chowder.

25 g unsalted butter

125 g rindless smoked bacon, chopped into 2.5 cm pieces

1 large onion, finely chopped

1 tablespoon plain flour

375 ml milk

500 ml chicken stock

250 g new potatoes, quartered lengthways

leaves from a bunch of watercress, chopped

freshly ground black pepper

serves 4

Put the butter into a large saucepan or wok and heat until melted. Add the bacon and cook over medium heat for 4–5 minutes until golden.

Add the onion and cook gently over low heat for about 10 minutes until softened and translucent. Add the flour and cook, stirring with a wooden spoon, for about 1 minute. Gradually add the milk and stock and bring to the boil, stirring constantly.

Add the potatoes and simmer for 10–12 minutes until tender when pierced with a knife. Stir in the watercress and sprinkle generously with pepper.

Ladle into soup bowls and serve.

rich red pepper and bean soup

Canned beans can form the basis of lots of filling, easy-to-make soups, salads and main courses, so keep several cans of each kind in your storecupboard.

2 large red peppers, halved, deseeded and cut into 1 cm slices

3 tablespoons olive oil

1 large onion, finely chopped

150 ml dry white wine

820 g canned butterbeans, drained and rinsed

700 ml vegetable stock

125 g fine green beans

salt and freshly ground black pepper

chilli or garlic oil, to serve

serves 4

Preheat the oven to 200°C (400°F) Gas 6. Put the peppers in a roasting tin, drizzle with 1 tablespoon olive oil and sprinkle with salt and pepper. Transfer to the preheated oven and roast for 30 minutes.

Heat the remaining oil in a large saucepan. Add the onion and cook over medium heat for 10 minutes, or until softened and translucent.

Add the wine to the onion and boil for 1 minute. Add the butterbeans

and stock and black pepper to taste. Bring to the boil, reduce the heat and simmer for 15 minutes.

Meanwhile, add the green beans to the peppers in the oven and roast for a further 8–10 minutes.

Transfer the butterbean mixture to a food processor or blender and blend until smooth. Ladle into soup plates or bowls, then top with a spoonful of the peppers and beans. Drizzle with the chilli or garlic oil and serve.

mediterranean fish stew

fish and seafood

There are so many varieties of wonderful fish and seafood – make the most of them! For maximum flavour and freshness, buy from your fishmonger and cook it the same day.

mediterranean fish stew

Prawn shells are full of flavour, which seeps into the sauce and contributes to its richness. Eat this dish with your fingers and mop up with plenty of crusty fresh bread.

1 large fennel bulb, with leafy tops

2 tablespoons olive oil

2 garlic cloves, crushed

200 ml dry white wine

300 ml fish stock

800 g canned chopped tomatoes

a pinch of sugar

250 g cherry tomatoes, halved

500 g monkfish fillet, cut into 4 cm chunks

12 mussels, scrubbed and beards removed (page 34)

12 large, unpeeled, uncooked prawns, heads removed

salt and freshly ground black pepper

to serve

extra virgin olive oil

pimento paste (page 144) (optional)

serves 4

Remove the leafy tops from the fennel bulb, chop them coarsely and set aside. Cut the bulb into quarters, remove and discard the core, then finely chop the bulb.

Heat the oil in a large saucepan or wok. Add the fennel bulb and fry for 5 minutes. Add the garlic and fry for a further 1 minute. Add the wine, stock, canned tomatoes and sugar and stir well. Bring to the boil, reduce the heat then simmer for 5 minutes. Add the cherry tomatoes and cook for a further 5 minutes. Add plenty of salt and freshly ground black pepper.

Add the monkfish and return to simmering. Stir in the mussels and prawns, cover and cook for about 5 minutes, or until the mussels have opened and the fish is cooked.

Ladle the stew into deep plates or bowls and spoon the pimento paste, if using, on top. Sprinkle with the fennel tops and olive oil and serve.

Variation Though not authentically Mediterranean, salmon is also delicious in this stew. Clams are good too, but can be sandy, so cook them in a separate saucepan and strain the liquid before adding them to the stew.

californian tuna noodle salad

californian tuna noodle salad

A light, aromatic dish. Be careful not to overcook the tuna – it should be rare – and don't forget that it will go on cooking even after you take it off the heat. The green vegetables are blanched and refreshed, as described on page 15, for best colour and texture.

juice of 1 lime
2 tablespoons olive oil
2 tablespoons teriyaki sauce
4 tuna steaks, 150 g each
200 g fine egg noodles, cooked and drained (page 21)
125 g sugar snap peas, blanched, refreshed (page 15)
   and halved lengthways
2 large carrots, finely cut into matchstick strips
125 g baby plum tomatoes, halved
4 baby bok choy, blanched and refreshed (page 15)
2 tablespoons toasted sesame seeds (page 11)
freshly ground black pepper

dressing
4 tablespoons sunflower oil
a bunch of spring onions, cut into chunky strips
3 tablespoons light soy sauce
freshly squeezed juice of 1 large orange
5 cm piece of fresh ginger, peeled and grated
1 large garlic clove, crushed
2 teaspoons sesame oil
salt and freshly ground black pepper

serves 4

Put the lime juice, olive oil and teriyaki sauce in a bowl and mix well. Put the tuna steaks in a shallow dish and pour over the teriyaki mixture. Sprinkle with black pepper, turn to coat and set aside for 30 minutes.

Meanwhile, to make the dressing, put 1 tablespoon of the sunflower oil in a frying pan and heat until hot. Add the spring onions and stir-fry for 30 seconds. Remove from the heat and stir in the remaining dressing ingredients. Add salt and pepper to taste.

Put the noodles, sugar snap peas, carrots and tomatoes into a mixing bowl. Add the warm dressing and toss gently until all the ingredients are well coated.

Heat a stove-top grill pan or frying pan until hot. Add the tuna steaks and sear for 1–2 minutes on each side. Remove from the pan and cut the steaks into slices. Pile a little of the noodle salad and bok choy onto each serving plate and sprinkle with the sesame seeds. Top with the seared tuna slices and serve at once.

Preparing seafood
• If using larger prawns, cut them down the back and pull out and discard the black thread. If the prawns are small, don't bother.
• Squid can be fiddly to clean yourself – get the fishmonger to do it for you, or buy it ready-cleaned from the supermarket.
• Scrub mussels and pull off the seaweedy 'beards'. Tap them against the kitchen bench – if they don't close, throw them away. After they're cooked, throw away any that haven't opened.

Cooking fish
• It's important not to overcook fish – cook it just until it becomes opaque all the way through.
• Remember it keeps cooking after you remove it from the pan.
• Tuna can be underdone (pink in the middle), but it must be very fresh. To make sure, buy it from a fishmonger.

marinated vodka salmon

This is salmon served ceviche-style — a method in which fish or seafood is 'cooked' by the citrus juice in its marinade. It is a popular way to eat seafood in Central and South America. Fresh fish is absolutely essential.

375 g salmon fillet

4 spring onions, finely sliced diagonally

1 red chilli, deseeded and finely chopped (page 43)

3 tablespoons vodka

juice of 2 limes

2 tablespoons extra virgin olive oil

leaves from a bunch of coriander

salt and freshly ground black pepper

black rye bread, to serve

serves 4

Put the salmon fillet on a board and cut it crossways into 1 cm slices. Arrange the salmon slices in overlapping layers on a large serving plate. Sprinkle with salt and freshly ground black pepper.

Put the spring onions, chilli, vodka and lime juice in a small bowl and mix well. Pour the mixture over the salmon and set aside for 30 minutes, to let the salmon 'cook'.

Sprinkle with salt and pepper and drizzle with the olive oil. Top with the coriander and serve with black rye bread.

trout fishcakes

I favour trout over salmon for making fishcakes, as it is moist and has a lovely, earthy flavour. The shaped cakes need to be chilled so they will keep their shape when fried.

500 g potatoes, cut into small chunks

½ teaspoon salt

500 g rainbow trout fillets

250 ml milk

25 g butter

a small bunch of flat leaf parsley, chopped

a small bunch of chives, chopped

flour, for shaping the fishcakes

1 egg, beaten

125 g fresh white breadcrumbs

sunflower oil, for frying

125 g fine green beans, blanched and refreshed (page 15)

125 g baby spinach leaves

salt and freshly ground black pepper

to serve (optional)

extra chives

tartare sauce

quick aioli (page 144)

lemon beurre blanc (page 145)

dijon dressing (page 145)

serves 4

Put the potatoes in a saucepan, cover with water and bring to the boil. Add the salt and simmer gently for 15 minutes, until the potatoes are tender.

Meanwhile, put the fish in a large, shallow saucepan and pour over the milk. Cover, bring to the boil, reduce the heat and simmer very gently for 5–6 minutes, until the fish is opaque all the way through and just cooked. Using a slotted spoon, remove to a plate and let cool. Remove and discard the skin, then coarsely flake the fish.

Drain the potatoes and return them to the pan. Add the butter and mash until smooth. Put into a large bowl, add the parsley and chives and mix. Add plenty of salt and black pepper. Using a large metal spoon, gently fold in the flaked fish.

Using floured hands, shape the mixture into 4 round cakes, about 2.5 cm thick. Dip them first into the beaten egg and then into the breadcrumbs to coat all over. Refrigerate for 30 minutes.

Put 2 cm oil into a large frying pan and heat until hot. Add the fishcakes and fry over a medium heat for 3–4 minutes on each side, until golden brown and heated through.

Toss the beans and spinach together in a bowl, divide between 4 plates and put a fishcake on top. Serve with extra chives and one of the sauces.

Frying fishcakes

Put enough oil in the pan for the food to cook evenly on both sides, allowing for some of the fat to be absorbed. This will avoid a 'tide mark' on the fishcakes. The level should be more than half way up the sides of the fishcakes.

chicken and duck

Chicken is a great favourite in our house and we are always revisiting old favourites as well as trying new ideas. Duck is popular too – don't save it for special occasions.

mexican chicken burgers

Chicken thighs have more flavour and are less dry than breast, so are ideal for these spicy burgers. Shape the burgers with wet hands, to stop the mixture sticking to them.

1 tablespoon olive oil, plus extra for brushing

1 small red onion, finely chopped

1 large garlic clove, crushed

2 teaspoons ground coriander

250 g boneless, skinless chicken thighs, each cut into 6

50 g breadcrumbs

15 g bottled jalapeño chillies, drained and rinsed

1 egg, beaten

salt and freshly ground black pepper

to serve

4 small wholemeal baps, halved crossways

salad leaves

chunky guacamole (page 143)

1 lime, cut into wedges

serves 4

Heat the oil in a small saucepan. Add the onion and fry for 5 minutes until softened. Add the garlic and ground coriander and cook for a further 1 minute. Let cool.

Transfer to a food processor and add the chicken, breadcrumbs, chillies, egg and some salt and pepper. Blend to a coarse paste.

Transfer the mixture from the food processor to a clean work surface. Using wet hands, shape the mixture into 4 burgers and refrigerate for 30 minutes.

Heat a stove-top grill pan until hot, brush with a little oil, add the burgers and fry gently for 6–7 minutes on each side until cooked through.

Put each burger in a bap with salad and Chunky Guacamole and serve with lime wedges.

coq au vin

This modern version of the classic dish of chicken cooked in wine is a handy short cut. Cutting slashes in the chicken lets the marinade soak into and flavour the meat, while keeping it tender and moist.

4 boneless, skinless chicken breasts
150 ml red wine
1 garlic clove, sliced
2 tablespoons olive oil
a sprig of thyme

sauce
20 g dried porcini mushrooms, rinsed thoroughly
1 tablespoon olive oil
6 shallots, halved
a pinch of sugar
125 g smoked bacon, chopped
1 garlic clove, crushed
2 teaspoons plain flour
150 ml red wine
150 ml port
a sprig of thyme, plus 4 sprigs to serve
salt and freshly ground black pepper

serves 4

Using a small, sharp knife, slash the top of each chicken breast in a criss-cross fashion, taking care not to cut all the way through. Put the breasts in a shallow dish. Add the red wine, garlic, oil and thyme and mix. Cover and refrigerate for 20 minutes. The chicken will absorb most of the marinade.

Meanwhile, to make the sauce, put the dried porcini in a bowl and cover with 150 ml boiling water. Let soak for 15 minutes, then drain, reserving the liquid. (The liquid can sometimes be gritty, so strain it through a tea strainer.) Coarsely chop the mushrooms.

Heat the oil in a frying pan. Add the shallots and sugar and fry for 10 minutes until golden. Add the bacon and garlic and fry for a further 5 minutes. Stir in the flour and cook for 1 minute. Add the mushrooms and their soaking liquid, red wine, port and a sprig of thyme. Bring to the boil, reduce the heat and simmer for 20 minutes until syrupy. Add salt and pepper to taste.

Meanwhile, heat a stove-top grill pan until hot. Transfer the chicken to the grill pan, discarding any remaining marinade. Cook for about 5 minutes on each side, until the chicken is cooked through, with no trace of pink in the middle. Serve with the sauce poured over, topped with a sprig of thyme.

Chicken cooking tips

• *It's important to cook chicken all the way through. To test, push a skewer or small sharp knife into the thickest part – this is normally the drumstick or thigh. The juices that run out should be clear or golden – if they are pink or bloody, you must cook it for longer.*
• *To check whether chicken breasts are cooked, cut one to see. Cut through the thickest part – it should be opaque all the way through, with no trace of blood.*
• *Boneless, skinless chicken is quick and easy to cook, but if you cook it with the skin on and the bone in, it will have more flavour. Skin keeps it moist, while the bone helps conduct heat.*

honeyed duck with mango salsa

honeyed duck with mango salsa

Duck always works well with fruit and this recipe is also good with nectarines. Pricking the duck skin stops it shrinking as it cooks, while the honey-soy mixture produces a delicious, crackly skin.

4 small to medium duck breasts, skin on

1 tablespoon soy sauce

1 tablespoon honey

salt

mango salsa

1 large, ripe mango

1 orange pepper, halved, deseeded and diced

6 spring onions, finely sliced

2 tablespoons olive oil

grated zest and juice of 1 orange

juice of 1 lime

4 sprigs of coriander

serves 4

Cut the sides off the mango in 4 slabs, from top to bottom, and discard the stone and surrounding flesh. With a small, sharp knife, cut a criss-cross pattern into the flesh of each piece, down to the skin. Push the skin with your thumbs to invert and scrape off the cubes of flesh with a knife.

Put the mango in a bowl with the remaining salsa ingredients and set aside to develop the flavours. Meanwhile, preheat the oven to 240°C (450°F) Gas 8.

Prick the duck skin all over with a fork and rub with a little salt. Transfer the duck breasts to a wire rack set over a roasting tin (this will allow the excess fat to drip away).

Put the soy sauce and honey into a small bowl and mix well. Spread the mixture over the duck skin. Transfer to the oven and roast for 15–20 minutes, until the duck is just cooked but still pink in the middle, and the skin well browned and crisp. Remove from the oven and let the duck rest for 5 minutes before carving.

Carve the duck breasts crossways into slices and serve with the mango salsa.

poussins with citrus baked rice

This delicious dish of mini chicken and rice is a cross between a paella and a risotto, with the rice cooking and swelling in the hot stock in the oven. Cooking the poussins breast side down gives you a lovely, moist breast, as the fat and juices from the legs will seep down into it. You still get a crisp, golden skin, when you turn them back to breast side up for the last stage of cooking.

4 poussins

4 garlic cloves, crushed

4 bay leaves

leaves from 2 sprigs of rosemary

3 unwaxed lemons, halved crossways

150 ml white wine

4 tablespoons virgin olive oil

2 large Spanish onions, sliced

2 teaspoons turmeric

500 g risotto rice, such as arborio or carnaroli

about 1 litre hot chicken stock

virgin olive oil, for roasting

salt and freshly ground black pepper

serves 4

Put the poussins in a large bowl and add plenty of salt and pepper. Rub with the garlic, sprinkle with the herbs, squeeze over the lemon juice and add the squeezed lemon halves to the bowl. Pour in the wine and half the oil. Cover and refrigerate for at least 2 hours, or overnight.

Preheat the oven to 200°C (400°F) Gas 6. Heat the remaining oil in a paella pan or large, heavy roasting tin. Add the onions and fry until softened. Add the turmeric and fry gently for 30 seconds. Add the rice and cook for 1 minute, stirring well.

Put the poussins, breast side down, on top of the rice. Pour the marinade juices and half the hot stock over the top.

Bring to the boil on top of the stove, then remove from the heat and cover the whole tin with foil. Transfer to the preheated oven and cook for 25 minutes.

Remove from the oven and discard the foil. Turn the poussins over and add the remaining stock to the tin. Brush the poussins with a little extra oil. Return the uncovered tin to the oven and cook for a further 30 minutes until the poussins and rice are cooked.

Note You may need to add extra stock to the tin if the rice starts to dry out. Check several times as it is cooking.

herbed seared lamb with
aubergine and courgette butter

herbed seared lamb with aubergine and courgette butter

Butterflying a leg of lamb opens it out flat, with no bones, to an even thickness. It's a good way to speed up the cooking time, and gives a larger surface area for searing and flavouring. Ask your butcher to butterfly the lamb for you.

1.8 kg leg of lamb, butterflied

8 garlic cloves, sliced

½ bottle red wine

3 tablespoons olive oil

grated zest of 1 lemon

2–3 sprigs of thyme

2–3 sprigs of rosemary

freshly ground black pepper

aubergine and courgette butter

2 medium aubergines, cut into 1 cm cubes

2 courgettes, cut into 1 cm cubes

5 tablespoons extra virgin olive oil

freshly squeezed lemon juice, to taste

salt and freshly ground black pepper

serves 4–6

Using a sharp knife, remove the excess fat and skin from the lamb. Cut small pockets into the flesh on both sides and stud each pocket with the garlic slices.

Put the wine, oil, lemon zest, thyme and rosemary in a large dish and sprinkle with pepper. Add the lamb, cover and refrigerate for at least 4 hours, preferably overnight.

Preheat the oven to 200°C (400°F) Gas 6. Put the aubergine and courgette cubes in a large roasting tin. Drizzle with 3 tablespoons of the oil and sprinkle with black pepper. Roast in the oven for 35–40 minutes until tender. Transfer to a plate and set aside. Reduce the oven temperature to 190°C (375°F) Gas 5.

Put the roasting tin over a high heat on top of the stove. Drain the lamb by tipping the marinade into a saucepan while you hold the lamb in the dish. Put the drained lamb in the hot roasting tin and sear for 5 minutes on each side to seal. Meanwhile, heat the marinade in the saucepan and boil for 2–3 minutes, to reduce. Pour the marinade over the lamb and top with the herb sprigs.

Transfer the lamb to the oven and roast for 20 minutes per 500 g for medium lamb – check after 15 minutes per 500 g for rare or after 25–30 minutes for well done. (Remember that thin pieces of meat will cook faster than thick ones – see page 79 for other roasting times.) Remove from the oven, cover with foil, and let rest for 10 minutes.

Put the vegetables and remaining oil into a food processor. Pulse to a coarse paste. Add salt, pepper, and lemon juice. Carve the lamb into thick slices and arrange on a platter. Serve with pan juices and the aubergine-courgette butter.

Marinated, seared, roasted, stir-fried or grilled – the list is endless! Meat is a great, versatile ingredient. My tip is to spend more and buy less of the best quality you can find.

peppered sage pork with pasta

When cooking pork without crackling, always cook it gently, or it will become tough.

2 sun-dried peppers
500 g pork fillet
8 sage leaves
250 g pappardelle or tagliatelle pasta
15 g butter
½ tablespoon olive oil
50 ml dry sherry
200 ml double cream
100 ml chicken stock
1 tablespoon chopped fresh sage
salt and freshly ground black pepper

serves 4

Soak the sun-dried peppers in boiling water according to the instructions on the packet. Drain and cut into about 5 cm pieces.

Slice the pork fillet diagonally into 8 pieces. Using the palm of your hand, gently flatten the pieces of pork into round, medallion shapes.

Using a small, sharp knife, make 2 cuts through the centre of each medallion. Thread a piece of sliced pepper through 1 cut and a sage leaf through the second cut of each medallion. Sprinkle with black pepper.

Cook the pasta in a saucepan of boiling, salted water, as directed on the packet, until cooked, or 'al dente'.

Meanwhile, heat the butter and oil in a non-stick frying pan until foaming. Add the pork medallions and fry over a gentle to medium heat for 4–5 minutes on each side until golden and cooked all the way through. Transfer to a warm plate, cover with foil and set aside.

Pour the sherry into the hot frying pan and boil for 30 seconds. Stir in the cream, stock and sage. Bring to the boil again, reduce the heat and simmer for 3–4 minutes. Add salt and pepper to taste.

Drain the pasta, return it to the warm saucepan and toss with half of the sauce. Divide between serving plates. Top with 2 pieces of pork. Drizzle with the remaining sauce and serve at once.

chile con carne wraps

Adding the bitter dark chocolate at the last minute adds a lovely richness – as well as a dash of Mexican authenticity – to the sauce and brings it all together.

1 tablespoon olive oil, plus extra for brushing
1 large onion, chopped
2 teaspoons crushed dried chillies
400 g canned red kidney beans, drained and rinsed
400 g canned chopped tomatoes
150 ml red wine
2 garlic cloves, crushed
4 flour tortillas
2 sirloin steaks, 250 g each
15 g plain chocolate (minimum 70 per cent cocoa solids), coarsely chopped
freshly ground black pepper
chilli oil, to drizzle

to serve
chunky guacamole (page 143)
150 ml sour cream
½ iceberg lettuce, finely shredded

serves 4

Heat the oil in a large saucepan. Add the onion and fry for 5–6 minutes until golden. Stir in the dried chillies, kidney beans, tomatoes, wine and garlic. Bring to the boil, reduce the heat and simmer for 15–20 minutes.

Heat a stove-top grill pan until very hot. Add the tortillas, one at a time, and cook for 1 minute on each side until lightly toasted. Put them in a very low oven to keep warm.

Brush the steaks with olive oil and sprinkle with freshly ground black pepper. Add the steaks to the grill pan and sear for 2–3 minutes on each side for medium rare, or about 1–2 minutes longer, depending on thickness, if you prefer your meat well done.

Remove from the pan and drizzle with the chilli oil. Let the meat rest for 5 minutes before cutting into diagonal slices. Meanwhile, stir the chocolate into the sauce.

Serve as a wrap in the warm tortillas, with Chunky Guacamole, sour cream and lettuce.

lemongrass and rosemary risotto
with orange roasted roots

vegetables

You'll find lots of vegetable dishes throughout this book, but most of the recipes in this section treat them as the main event – as a course in themselves.

lemongrass and rosemary risotto with orange roasted roots

Always add liquid to a risotto gradually so that the rice absorbs it little by little, as it swells and cooks. The stock should go in hot, so put it in a saucepan over a low heat and ladle it in as you go.

2 tablespoons olive oil

1 large onion, finely chopped

1 stalk of lemongrass

a large sprig of rosemary, plus extra to serve

375 g risotto rice, such as arborio or carnaroli

300 ml white wine

about 850 ml hot vegetable stock

1 tablespoon chopped fresh rosemary

salt and freshly ground black pepper

1 recipe orange roasted roots (page 84), to serve

serves 4

Put the oil into a large saucepan and heat. When hot, add the onion and fry for 5–8 minutes until softened and turning golden.

Using a rolling pin, lightly bruise the lemongrass and the sprig of rosemary to release the flavours. Add to the onion, then add the rice and cook, stirring continuously, for 1 minute.

Add the wine, 1 ladle of hot stock and salt and freshly ground black pepper to taste. Bring to the boil, then reduce the heat to simmering. As the stock is absorbed, gradually add more, 1 ladle at a time, letting each be absorbed before adding the next.

Cook for about 20 minutes, stirring frequently, until the rice is cooked through. Stir in the chopped rosemary and salt and pepper to taste.

Pile the risotto onto 4 large plates or bowls. Top with the hot root vegetables and a sprig of rosemary, then serve.

creamy scalloped potatoes and parsnips

This is one of my all-time favourites, and yes, it does need all that cream!

425 ml double cream

300 ml milk

2 garlic cloves, crushed

freshly grated nutmeg

1 bay leaf

500 g potatoes, finely sliced

500 g parsnips, finely sliced

salt and freshly ground black pepper

a shallow, medium ovenproof dish, lightly buttered

serves 4

Preheat the oven to 170°C (325°F) Gas 3. Put the cream, milk, garlic, nutmeg to taste and bay leaf into a saucepan with salt and pepper to taste. Heat gently to just below boiling point, then remove from the heat.

Arrange layers of potatoes and parsnips in the prepared dish. Pour in the cream mixture. Cover with foil and cook in the preheated oven for 45 minutes. Remove the foil and cook in the oven for about 30 minutes more, until golden.

mushroom, leek and
thyme puff pies

mushroom, leek and thyme puff pies

Add the cream cheese to the leeks and mushrooms only after they have cooled, or the cheese will melt and make the filling runny. Make sure you wash the leeks thoroughly, to remove any dirt or grit between the layers.

25 g butter
2 leeks, washed and finely sliced diagonally
250 g flat, open mushrooms, finely sliced
1 large garlic clove, crushed
200 g cream cheese
flour, for dusting
2 tablespoons thyme leaves
375 g ready-rolled puff pastry
1 egg, beaten with a pinch of salt
salt and freshly ground black pepper

serves 4

Heat half the butter in a large frying pan or wok until melted. Add the leeks and fry for about 5 minutes until softened. Transfer to a large bowl.

Add the remaining butter to the frying pan and heat until melted. Add the mushrooms and garlic and cook for 5 minutes until softened and the juices have evaporated. Add to the leeks with plenty of salt and pepper and let cool. When completely cool, add the cream cheese and mix well.

Dust a work surface with flour and sprinkle with the thyme. Put the pastry on top of the thyme and roll out to a square, about 32 cm. Turn the pastry over. Using a large, sharp knife, cut into 4 smaller squares.

Spoon the mixture onto one side of each square leaving a 1 cm border at the edges. Brush the border with a little water, then fold the pastry over the filling. Press the edges lightly together and use the back of a fork to seal the edges. Brush with the beaten egg to glaze and then, using a sharp knife, cut a small slit in each to let air escape. Transfer to a baking sheet, cover and refrigerate for 30 minutes.

Meanwhile, preheat the oven to 200°C (400°F) Gas 6. Transfer the pies to the oven and bake for 25–30 minutes until risen and golden brown.

Vegetable tips
• *Buy small quantities and buy often.*
• *Don't keep tomatoes in the refrigerator – keep them at room temperature. Don't keep potatoes in the refrigerator either – keep them in a cool, dark place, such as a kitchen drawer or cupboard.*
• *Store other vegetables in the refrigerator to keep them fresh.*
• *When peeling most vegetables, use a peeler not a knife (though for hard-skinned vegetables like turnip, you will need a knife).*
• *When cutting vegetables to be boiled, cut into evenly-sized pieces so they will all be cooked at the same time – this is very important for broccoli, cauliflower and potatoes.*
• *Scrub organic vegetables, but peel any that aren't organic.*

vegetable goulash

Paprika gives Hungarian goulash its appealing reddish colour and fragrance. Here the smoked variety, often used in Spanish cookery, adds a distinctive, deep flavour.

2 tablespoons olive oil

1 large onion, chopped

1 heaped teaspoon brown sugar

3 garlic cloves, crushed

5 dried birdseye chillies, soaked in boiling water to cover

3 tablespoons smoked sweet paprika

1 large parsnip, cut into 2.5 cm cubes

1 large potato, cubed

200 g baby carrots, trimmed and halved lengthways

800 g canned chopped tomatoes

about 300 ml red wine

410 g canned chickpeas, drained and rinsed

freshly ground black pepper

to serve

2 tablespoons Greek yoghurt or sour cream

a bunch of mint, coarsely chopped

lemon and cumin cracked wheat (right) or cooked rice (page 22)

serves 4

Put the oil in a large saucepan and heat. When hot, add the onions, cover with a lid and cook over medium heat for 10–15 minutes until softened. Remove the lid and stir in the sugar. Increase the heat to high and cook for a further 5 minutes until golden.

Add the garlic, drained chillies and paprika and cook for 30 seconds. Add all the vegetables, tomatoes and wine with 300 ml water. Bring to the boil, reduce the heat and simmer, uncovered, for 35–40 minutes until the vegetables are just tender, adding a little extra water if they dry out. Add the chickpeas and plenty of black pepper and simmer for a further 5–10 minutes.

Transfer to serving plates and drizzle with the yoghurt or sour cream. Sprinkle with the mint and serve with Lemon and Cumin Cracked Wheat or rice.

lemon and cumin cracked wheat

Cracked wheat is similar to bulgar wheat. Used often in Middle Eastern cookery, it is excellent served cold in salads or hot with chicken or vegetable dishes.

300 g bulgar wheat

2 tablespoons virgin olive oil

1 unwaxed lemon, finely chopped

3 teaspoons ground cumin

2 garlic cloves, crushed

freshly ground black pepper

serves 4

Put the bulgar wheat in a bowl and add boiling water to cover. Leave to swell for 15–20 minutes until soft, then drain through a sieve, pressing out any excess water.

Heat the oil in a large saucepan. Add the lemon and fry for 2 minutes, then add the cumin and garlic and fry briefly for 30 seconds. Add the bulgar wheat and stir-fry for a further 1–2 minutes. Add plenty of pepper, then serve.

vegetable goulash with lemon and cumin cracked wheat

luxury hoummus

dressings
dips and sauces

Dips, dressings and sauces all bring a meal to life – so dip, dunk and mix away.

luxury hoummus

You can really taste the difference in homemade hoummus, especially this deluxe, caper-topped version.

1 can chickpeas, about 410 g, drained and rinsed

3 tablespoons tahini paste

2 garlic cloves, coarsely chopped

freshly squeezed juice of 1 lemon

4 tablespoons extra virgin olive oil, plus extra to drizzle

a large bunch of flat leaf parsley, coarsely chopped

2 tablespoons capers, rinsed and drained

½ teaspoon crushed dried chillies

salt and freshly ground black pepper

to serve

pita bread, toasted

1 lemon, cut into wedges

serves 4 as a starter

Put the chickpeas, tahini paste and garlic in a food processor and blend until smooth. Add the lemon juice, with 3 tablespoons of the oil and 1 tablespoon boiling water. Process until very smooth. Add plenty of salt and black pepper.

Put the parsley, capers, dried chillies and the remaining olive oil into a bowl and mix well.

Put a mound of the hoummus on each toasted pita bread and top with a spoonful of the parsley-caper mixture. Drizzle with olive oil and serve with lemon wedges.

rocket salsa verde

Salsa verde is a raw, green and extremely versatile sauce – great with fish and meat. This is just one of many variations.

50 g wild rocket, coarsely chopped

½ bunch chives, coarsely chopped

4 tablespoons extra virgin olive oil

salt and freshly ground black pepper

serves 4

Put the rocket in a blender, add the chives, olive oil and 2 tablespoons water. Blend until smooth. Add salt and pepper to taste, then serve. Refrigerate for up to 1 day.

Note If you don't have a regular, bench-top blender, a small, inexpensive stick blender is fine.

chunky guacamole

Use avocados which are just ripe – overripe ones taste bitter and rancid.

2 large ripe avocados, halved, pitted, peeled and cut into 1 cm cubes

freshly squeezed juice of 1 lime

2 shallots, finely chopped

8 cherry tomatoes, quartered

1 large red chilli, deseeded and finely chopped (page 43)

1 garlic clove, finely chopped

a pinch of sugar

1 tablespoon extra virgin olive oil

salt and freshly ground black pepper

serves 4

Put the avocado in a bowl and pour over the lime juice. Add the remaining ingredients to the bowl with a little salt and lots of freshly ground black pepper. Mix well.

To serve as a starter, fill 4 teacups with the relish and turn them out into a mound on the centre of each serving plate. Drizzle with oil and sprinkle with black pepper.

fresh red pepper jam

pimento paste

fresh red pepper jam

Superb with pasta or on top of toasted bread with shavings of cheese.

2 tablespoons olive oil

2 red peppers, halved, deseeded and
finely sliced

2 yellow peppers, halved, deseeded and
finely sliced

2 orange peppers, halved, deseeded and
finely sliced

1 red chilli, halved, deseeded (page 43)
and finely sliced diagonally

2 garlic cloves, peeled

1 tablespoon sugar

1 lemon, halved

salt and freshly ground black pepper

serves 4

Heat the oil in a large saucepan. Add the peppers, chilli, garlic and sugar. Squeeze the lemon juice into the pan, then add the squeezed halves. Stir.

Put a piece of wet, crumpled greaseproof paper on top of the mixture in the pan and cover with a lid. Cook gently over a low heat for 35–40 minutes until the peppers are

meltingly soft. Remove the paper from the pan and increase the heat to reduce the liquid for about 3–4 minutes. Add salt and pepper to taste and remove from the heat. When cool, transfer to sterilized jars (below). Keep refrigerated and use within 1–2 weeks.

quick aioli

A short-cut, easy version of this garlic flavoured mayonnaise.

2 garlic cloves, crushed

6 tablespoons mayonnaise

2 tablespoons crème fraîche or
Greek yoghurt

2 tablespoons flat leaf parsley, chopped

salt and freshly ground black pepper

serves 4

Sterilizing jars

Put the jars in a saucepan and fill the pan with water to cover the jars. Bring to the boil, reduce the heat slightly and boil gently for 10 minutes. Remove and let drain on kitchen paper until dry.

Put the ingredients in a bowl and stir to mix. Keep refrigerated and use within 2 days.

pimento paste

Based on the classic French *rouille*, traditionally served with fish soup.

2 large red peppers

1 tablespoon olive oil

25 g white bread, crusts removed,
soaked in a little water and excess
squeezed out

2 garlic cloves, crushed

1 teaspoon cayenne pepper

100 ml extra virgin olive oil

salt and freshly ground black pepper

serves 4

Preheat the oven to 200°C (400°F) Gas 6. Put the peppers in a roasting tin and drizzle with the oil.

Roast in the oven for 35–40 minutes, turning them occasionally, until slightly blackened all over. Put the peppers in a large plastic food bag, seal and let cool. The steam released will loosen the skins.

Remove the peppers from the bag, reserving any juices. Peel off the skin, cut in half and remove the seeds. Put the pepper halves in a food processor with the bread, garlic, cayenne and pepper juices and blend until smooth. With the motor running, slowly add the olive oil. Add salt and black pepper to taste. Keep refrigerated and use within 2 days.

red onion marmalade

Delicious in burgers, with sausages and cold meat, or on bruschetta with goats' cheese (page 64).

2 tablespoons olive oil
750 g red onions, very thinly sliced
1 bay leaf
1 teaspoon thyme leaves
50 g demerara sugar
3 tablespoons balsamic vinegar
150 ml red wine
grated zest and juice of 1 orange
salt and freshly ground black pepper

serves 8

Heat the oil in a large saucepan until hot. Add the onions, bay leaf and thyme and salt and black pepper to taste. Cover with a lid and cook over a low heat, stirring occasionally, for 30 minutes until the onions are softened and translucent.

Add the sugar, vinegar, red wine and the orange zest and juice. Cook uncovered for a further 1½ hours until no liquid is left and the onions are a dark, rich, red colour. Stir frequently during the last 30 minutes to stop the onions burning.

Let the mixture cool, then transfer to sterilized jars (see opposite). It will keep refrigerated for several weeks.

roquefort sauce

Wonderful as a dip with celery and breadsticks, on burgers or with chicken cooked in the grill pan.

100 g Roquefort cheese
200 g Greek yoghurt
freshly ground black pepper

serves 4

Put the Roquefort in a bowl and coarsely crush with a fork. Stir in the yoghurt and sprinkle with black pepper. If the yoghurt is quite thick, you may need to add 1–2 tablespoons of cold water.

lemon beurre blanc

A lighter, lemon version of the classic French butter sauce – perfect with fish.

2 shallots, finely chopped
4 black peppercorns
2 parsley stalks
250 ml white wine
1 tablespoon white wine vinegar
6 tablespoons double cream
50 g unsalted butter, diced and chilled
freshly squeezed lemon juice
salt and freshly ground black pepper

serves 4

Put the shallots, peppercorns, parsley stalks, wine and vinegar in a medium saucepan. Bring to the boil, reduce the heat and simmer until the mixture has reduced by half. Add the cream and simmer for 1–2 minutes.

Reduce the heat to very low and gently whisk in the chilled butter. Pass the sauce through a sieve and add salt, pepper and lemon juice to taste. Keep it warm until needed.

dijon dressing

A simple all-purpose dressing for salads. You can adjust this as much as you like – try wholegrain mustard in place of smooth, and experiment with different vinegars – sherry, cider, red wine or even Japanese rice vinegar.

1 tablespoon smooth Dijon mustard
1 tablespoon white wine vinegar
4 tablespoons extra virgin olive oil
1 garlic clove, crushed
salt and freshly ground black pepper

serves 4

Put the mustard, vinegar, oil and garlic in a bowl and mix with a fork or small metal whisk. Add enough water for the consistency you want – about 1–2 tablespoons – and salt and black pepper to taste.

dijon dressing

mini pavlovas
with hot sugared plums

Pavlova is a type of meringue, with a gooey middle that you get by adding cornflour and vinegar to regular meringue mixture. Traditionally, the meringue case is filled with cream and fresh fruit, but hot plums and ice cream make a fabulous variation. I also think it is more fun to serve little individual ones, which look prettier. You can make the meringue part up to a day in advance.

pavlovas

3 egg whites

175 g caster sugar

1 teaspoon cornflour

½ teaspoon white wine vinegar

plums

500 g plums, about 8, halved and pitted

1 teaspoon ground cinnamon

40 g caster sugar

15 g butter

to serve

vanilla ice cream

4 sprigs of mint

a baking sheet, lined with parchment paper

serves 4

Preheat the oven to 140°C (275°F) Gas 1.

Put the egg whites into a clean bowl and, using an electric whisk, whisk until stiff. Gradually whisk in the sugar, until the mixture is very stiff. Sift in the cornflour, then, using a large metal spoon, fold in with the vinegar.

Divide the mixture into 4 mounds on the parchment. Using a dessert spoon, flatten to a disc shape, making a light indent in the middle of each. Bake in the preheated oven for about 30–40 minutes until the meringue is hard and the baking parchment peels away from the bottom of the

pavlovas. Cool on a wire rack. You can make up to 1 day in advance and store in an airtight container.

Increase the oven to 200°C (400°F) Gas 6. Put the plums, cut side up, on a baking sheet. Put the cinnamon and sugar in a bowl, mix and sprinkle over the plums. Divide the butter between the plums, transfer to the oven and bake for 15–20 minutes until golden and bubbling hot.

Put the pavlovas onto small plates and top with a few scoops of vanilla ice cream. Put the hot plums beside the pavlovas and decorate with mint sprigs.

peach marsala trifle

Based on Italian tiramisù, with the added bonus of plenty of fruit. No jelly in sight!

300 ml strong black coffee

200 ml Marsala wine

115 g sponge fingers

4 ripe peaches or nectarines, halved and pitted

250 g mascarpone cheese

25 g caster sugar

300 ml double cream

cocoa powder, for dusting

serves 6

Put the coffee and 150 ml of the Marsala into a shallow serving dish. Dip each sponge finger into the coffee mixture and use to line the base of the dish. Cut the peaches or nectarines into thin slices and arrange in layers over the sponge fingers.

Put the mascarpone and sugar into a large bowl and beat with a wooden spoon until soft. Gently beat in the cream and the remaining Marsala.

Spoon the mascarpone mixture over the peaches and, using a spatula, smooth to cover the fruit. Dust generously with cocoa powder. Cover and refrigerate for 2 hours to let the flavours soak into each other, then serve.

I think there's nothing to beat a homemade pudding – everyone loves them and making something simple and delicious can be very easy and quick.

sweet things

cherry almond tart

cherry almond tart

Canned Morello cherries have a wonderful sweet-sour flavour, but fresh cherries or ripe, sliced nectarines are a good substitute if you can't find them. The preheated baking sheet gives a crisp base, as its even heat cooks the pastry from underneath.

375 g ready-to-roll sweet or shortcrust pastry
100 g unsalted butter
100 g caster sugar
2 eggs, beaten
2 tablespoons brandy
100 g ground almonds
2 tablespoons plain flour
350 g canned Morello cherries, drained
icing sugar, for dusting
double cream or vanilla ice cream, to serve

a fluted tart tin, 25 cm diameter
a baking sheet

serves 6–8

Put a baking sheet in the oven and preheat to 200°C (400°F) Gas 6.

Roll out the pastry to just bigger than the tart tin. Carefully roll it around the rolling pin and drape over the tart tin. Press the pastry gently into the tin and, using a knife, trim off any pastry hanging over the edges. Prick the base lightly with a fork, then cover and refrigerate.

Meanwhile, put the butter and sugar in a bowl. Using an electric whisk, beat until pale and creamy. Gradually beat in the eggs, then stir in the brandy, almonds and flour.

Spread the mixture evenly over the pastry case and gently push the cherries at regular intervals into the surface. Put the tart onto the preheated baking sheet in the oven and bake for 10–15 minutes until the pastry begins to turn golden. Reduce the oven temperature to 180°C (350°F) Gas 4 and continue baking for a further 30–35 minutes until golden and cooked.

Let cool slightly, then remove from the tin and dust lightly with icing sugar. Cut into wedges and serve with cream or ice cream.

Cheat's pastry
• *Supermarkets sell most kinds of pastry in ready-to-roll form.*
• *Use sweet shortcrust pastry for sweet pies and all the other kinds of pastry for just about anything.*

hot tropical fruit parcels

If you fancy a kick of alcohol, add a spoonful of white rum to each parcel before sealing and baking.

2 large oranges
2 large ripe mangoes
4 passionfruit
4 teaspoons caster sugar
1 lime, quartered lengthways
coconut and lime ice cream (page 150)
  or vanilla ice cream, to serve

4 rectangles of foil, 30 x 20 cm each

serves 4

Preheat the oven to 200°C (400°F) Gas 6. Split the oranges into segments over a bowl, catching any juice in the bowl. Cut chunks from the mango and peel off the skin. Cut the passionfruit in half and scoop out the pulp. Add the sugar, mango chunks, orange segments and passionfruit pulp to the bowl and mix gently.

Divide the fruit between the foil rectangles, spooning over the remaining juice. Top each with a lime quarter.

Scrunch the foil together to seal and transfer to a baking sheet or tray. Cook in the oven for 6–8 minutes.

Put each parcel on a plate for everyone to open their own. Serve the ice cream separately.

coconut and lime ice cream

You don't need an ice cream maker to make ice cream, just an ordinary freezer and a shallow container. If your ice cream is rock solid, transfer it from the freezer to the refrigerator twenty minutes before serving so that it can soften slightly.

425 ml canned coconut cream
4 egg yolks
115 g caster sugar
grated zest of 2 limes

serves 4

Put the coconut cream into a non-stick saucepan over medium heat. Heat slowly to just below boiling point, then remove from the heat.

Meanwhile, put the egg yolks and sugar into a bowl and, using an electric whisk, whisk until pale and thick.

Slowly pour the hot coconut cream into the egg mixture, whisking continuously.

Wipe out the saucepan with kitchen paper and pour in the coconut and egg mixture. Return to medium heat and cook very gently, stirring continuously with a wooden spoon, until it thickens. Make sure it doesn't boil, or the mixture will curdle.

Pour into a bowl and let cool to room temperature.

Stir the lime zest into the cooled mixture, then pour into an ice cream maker and churn until frozen. If you don't have an ice cream maker, pour the mixture into a shallow metal or plastic container and put it into the freezer until half frozen, then remove from the freezer, whisk and return it to the freezer until solid.

Fresh fruit for pudding
* *Remember that fresh fruit makes a quick and easy end to a meal, even something as simple as orange wedges.*
* *In Greece, chunks and slices of fresh fruit are arranged in a dish of crushed ice and lime or lemon juice squeezed over the top.*
* *Prepare fruit in easily manageable sizes and keep it casual — life's too short to learn how to eat a grape with a knife and fork!*
* *Some fruits turn brown when exposed to air — apples and pears for instance. To stop this, brush the cut surfaces with lemon juice.*

hot whisky pancakes with raspberries

You can make the pancakes for this heartwarming pudding ahead of time — keep them in the refrigerator for up to two days, separated by squares of greaseproof paper. Alternatively, freeze them once they have cooled and remove from the freezer thirty minutes before using.

55 g plain flour
a pinch of salt
1 egg
150 ml milk
2 teaspoons peanut oil
300 ml freshly squeezed orange juice
2 tablespoons honey
15 g butter
3 tablespoons whisky
175 g fresh raspberries
icing sugar, to dust
cream or Greek yoghurt, to serve

serves 4

Sift the flour and salt into a large bowl. Make a well in the centre and crack the egg into the well. Gradually whisk in the milk to form a smooth batter.

Heat a medium, non-stick frying pan. Add a little oil and wipe out with kitchen paper. Pour enough batter into the pan to coat the base, then cook for about 1 minute. Loosen the edges with a long-handled turner, flip the pancake and cook for 1 minute more. Transfer to a plate and repeat with the remaining mixture to make 3 more pancakes. Set aside.

Pour the orange juice into the frying pan and add the honey and butter. Bring to the boil, reduce the heat and simmer for 5 minutes to concentrate the flavours and thicken the sauce slightly. Stir in the whisky.

Carefully fold each pancake in half, then in half again to make a triangle, and slide them into the simmering sauce. Heat for 30 seconds to warm through.

Transfer the pancakes and sauce to a serving plate and sprinkle with raspberries. Dust lightly with icing sugar and serve with cream or Greek yoghurt.

pecan mocha brownies

pecan mocha brownies

Brownies make an easy pudding. Serve them warm, straight from the oven, with a dollop of extra thick cream and a handful of raspberries. Alternatively, let them cool and eat them any time of day. Don't overcook brownies – they should be slightly gooey in the middle.

115 g unsalted butter

170 g caster sugar

1 teaspoon vanilla essence

2 eggs, beaten

55 g plain flour

55 g cocoa powder

1 teaspoon baking powder

55 g pecan nuts, coarsely chopped

40 g plain chocolate (minimum 70 per cent cocoa solids), coarsely chopped

2 teaspoons instant coffee, dissolved in 2 tablespoons boiling water

a cake tin, 18 cm square, greased, lined with greaseproof paper and lightly buttered

makes 9

Preheat the oven to 180°C (350°F) Gas 4.

Put the butter and sugar into a large bowl and, using an electric whisk, beat together until pale and fluffy. Add the vanilla and gradually beat in the eggs.

Sift the flour, cocoa powder and baking powder into the butter mixture and, using a large metal spoon, gently fold to mix. Fold in the pecans, chocolate and coffee. Spoon the mixture into the prepared tin and level out the top with the back of the spoon.

Transfer to the preheated oven and bake for about 30–35 minutes until just firm on top. If not eating immediately, leave in the tin for 10 minutes, then remove from the tin and transfer to a wire rack to cool. Cut into squares and serve.

brandied truffle curls

You need to make these quickly, while the mixture is still quite firm from the refrigerator. But don't be too precious – they look much better if they aren't all perfect!

200 g plain chocolate (minimum 70 per cent cocoa solids)

150 ml double cream

2 tablespoons brandy or whisky

55 g unsalted butter, softened (room temperature)

25 g cocoa powder

makes about 30

Put the chocolate and cream in a heatproof bowl set over a saucepan of simmering water and gently heat until the chocolate is just melted. Remove from the heat and stir in the brandy or whisky. Set aside for 5 minutes, then beat in the butter. Let cool, then transfer to the refrigerator and leave until the mixture has slightly hardened.

Sift the cocoa powder onto a plate. Draw a teaspoon across the truffle mixture, pressing slightly to pick up the mixture in the scoop of the spoon and to form curls. Dip them into the sifted cocoa, put on a large serving plate and refrigerate until needed.

hot chocolate fondue

A fabulous dipping sauce, as well as an excellent hot topping for ice cream. Alternatively, let it cool and thicken and spread it between two layers of sponge cake.

200 g dark chocolate, coarsely chopped

40 g unsalted butter

150 ml double cream

3 tablespoons brandy

150 ml boiling water

for dipping

4 baby bananas, peeled

1 small pineapple, peeled and cut into chunks

125 g black grapes

2 ripe pears, cut into slices

250 g large strawberries

1 loaf brioche bread or small panettone, cut into 3 cm cubes

serves 4

Put the chocolate, butter and cream into a heatproof bowl set over a saucepan of simmering water. Gently heat until melted and smooth. Remove from the heat and stir in the brandy and water. Transfer to a fondue pot or warm saucepan. Serve with fruits and breads for dipping.

drinks

Hot and frothy, long and cool and some with a bit of a kick! This chapter has drinks for every occasion – try a brandied hot chocolate on your own, or round up your friends for a big, cold jug of Sea Breeze or Sangría.

very berry smoothie

The Greek yoghurt in this bright, summery smoothie adds a creamy taste and colour to the red berries. Add more or less honey, depending on how sweet you like your smoothies.

125 g strawberries, hulled
125 g raspberries
50 g blueberries
200 ml cranberry juice
4 tablespoons Greek yoghurt
1 teaspoon runny honey
4 large ice cubes

serves 2

Put 2 tall glasses in the freezer to chill.

Put all the ingredients in a blender or food processor and work until almost smooth. Taste for sweetness, adding more honey if needed. Pour into the 2 chilled glasses and serve immediately.

tropical smoothie

Try to find a ripe and juicy mango to make this smoothie – it should be really fragrant. Peeling and slicing mangoes is quite a messy process, but absolutely worth it!

1 ripe mango
1 ripe banana, coarsely chopped
grated zest and juice of 1 lime
60 ml freshly squeezed orange juice

serves 2

To slice the mango, cut off both sides of the fruit either side of the stone. Peel back the skin and, at the same time, scoop out the flesh with a spoon. Cut into slices. Peel off the remaining skin from the mango and, using a knife, cut as much flesh as you can from the stone.

Put the bananas, mango slices, lime zest and juice and orange juice in a blender or food processor and work until smooth. Pour into glasses and serve at once.

irish coffee

8 tablespoons Irish whiskey
4 teaspoons light muscovado sugar
1 cafetière of fresh hot coffee (4-cup size)
150 ml double cream, lightly whipped
white chocolate truffles, to serve (optional)

serves 4

Put 2 tablespoons whiskey and 1 teaspoon sugar in each cup and stir. Add the hot coffee and stir briefly. Top with a generous spoonful of the cream and serve immediately, with chocolate truffles, if using.

amaretto iced cappuccino

A deluxe version of iced coffee, with a shot of Amaretto liqueur to make it extra special. Dunk the biscotti and let them soak up the creamy, almondy, coffee flavours.

4 scoops good quality vanilla ice cream
300 ml espresso coffee, freshly brewed
4 tablespoons Amaretto liqueur
biscotti biscuits, to serve

serves 2

Divide the vanilla ice cream between two extra large coffee cups. Put the coffee and Amaretto in a jug, mix, then pour over the ice cream. Serve immediately with the biscotti.

caffè frappè

Iced coffee really hits the spot on hot summer days, when you need a boost of caffeine as well as a refreshing, cool and creamy drink.

1 cafetière of fresh coffee (4-cup size), cooled
2 tablespoons caster sugar
150 ml double or single cream
4 tablespoons milk

serves 2

Pour the cooled coffee into an ice-cube tray, put in the freezer and freeze until almost solid.

Put the coffee ice cubes in a food processor with the sugar and process until coarsely chopped. Add the cream and milk and process until very finely chopped. Add more sugar as needed. Serve immediately in tall, chilled glasses.

brandied hot chocolate

The ultimate winter indulgence! One to sip from the comfort of a big armchair in front of a glowing fire.

250 ml semi-skimmed milk
45 g chocolate (minimum 70 per cent cocoa solids), grated
1 teaspoon sugar
2 tablespoons brandy
lightly whipped double cream, to serve (optional)

serves 1

Put the milk into a saucepan and heat to just below boiling point. Add the chocolate and sugar and stir over a very low heat until the chocolate has melted. Stir in the brandy and then pour into a mug. If you are feeling indulgent, finish with a spoonful of cream.

sea breeze

200 ml vodka
500 ml cranberry juice
300 ml grapefruit juice
ice cubes
1 lime, cut into wedges, to serve

serves 4

Put the vodka, cranberry juice and grapefruit juice into a large jug and mix well. Half fill 4 large glasses with ice, then pour the mixture over the ice. Top with a wedge of lime and serve immediately.

margarita

1 lime, cut into 6 wedges
coarsely ground salt
250 ml best quality tequila
75 ml Cointreau or Triple Sec
150 ml freshly squeezed lime juice, about 5–6 limes
3–4 tablespoons sugar, or to taste

serves 4

To salt-rim the glasses, rub a lime wedge around the rim of each glass. Put the salt on a small plate and dip each glass into the salt. Freeze until needed.

Pour the tequila, Cointreau, lime juice and sugar into a blender or food processor half-filled with ice. Process until the ice is finely chopped and the mixture becomes frothy. Taste for sweetness, adding more sugar if necessary. Pour into the chilled glasses and serve with a wedge of lime.

sangría

1 bottle rosé wine, 750 ml
600 ml cloudy lemonade
600 ml freshly squeezed orange juice
freshly squeezed juice of 2 lemons
150 ml brandy
2 oranges, sliced or cut into small wedges
2 lemons, sliced or cut into small wedges
ice cubes, to serve

serves 6–8

Put the wine, lemonade, orange juice, lemon juice and brandy into a very large jug or 2 small ones and mix. Add the orange and lemon slices and top up with plenty of ice. Serve in large, chilled wine glasses.

bloody mary

200 ml vodka
850 ml tomato juice
2 teaspoons horseradish sauce (optional)
1 tablespoon Tabasco, or to taste
2 tablespoons Worcestershire sauce
1 teaspoon celery salt
freshly ground black pepper

to serve
ice cubes
4 celery stalks
1 lemon, cut into 4 wedges

serves 4

Put all the ingredients in a large jug and mix. Add black pepper to taste. Pour into 4 large glasses half filled with ice. Serve with a stalk of celery and a wedge of lemon.

index

A

aioli, 144
lemon spatchcocked chicken, 71
almonds: cherry almond tart, 149
amaretto iced cappuccino, 156
apples, butter-baked, 82
aubergines: aubergine steaks with feta salad, 71
herbed seared lamb with aubergine and courgette butter, 135
avocados: chunky guacamole, 143
hot crunchy croutons with smoked bacon and avocado, 113
seared swordfish with avocado and salsa, 71

B

bacon: bean and bacon ragout with rosemary, 90
French toast with smoky bacon and spiked tomatoes, 108–9
hot crunchy croutons with smoked bacon and avocado, 113
trout with tarragon and bacon, 68
watercress and bacon chowder, 120
baking, 95–101
bananas: tropical smoothie, 154
barbecued steak with sizzled prawns, 72
barbecued corn with chilli butter, 68
barbecues, 67–73
basil: fried tomatoes with green pistou, 52
hot tomato and basil chutney, 109
beans: bean and bacon ragout with rosemary, 90
chile con carne wraps, 136
rich red pepper and bean soup, 121
beansprouts: tuna carpaccio salad, 117
beef: barbecued steak with sizzled prawns, 72
beef braised in red wine with light Gruyère dumplings, 92
chile con carne wraps, 136
roasting, 79
seared peppered beef salad with horseradish dressing, 114
berry puddings, hot boozy, 72
blanching, 15
bloody Mary, 157
blueberry and cinnamon frittata with maple syrup, 111
boiling, 14–23
braising, 87–93
brandied hot chocolate, 156
brandy: brandied truffle curls, 153
sangría, 157
bread: baking, 95
French toast with smoky bacon and spiked tomatoes, 108–9
Gorgonzola and walnut bread, 99
hot crunchy croutons with smoked bacon and avocado, 113
pan-grilled bruschetta with red onion marmalade and goats' cheese, 64

bresaola, rocket and Parmesan pizza topping, 98
broccoli trees with pan-fried pine nuts, 39
brownies, pecan mocha, 153
bruschetta: pan-grilled bruschetta with red onion marmalade and goats' cheese, 64
sweet tea-time bruschetta, 65
bulgar wheat: lemon and cumin cracked wheat, 141
burgers, Mexican chicken, 128
butter-baked apples, 82

C

cakes: baking, 95
crusted lime polenta cake, 100
pecan mocha brownies, 153
Californian tuna noodle salad, 124
cannellini beans: bean and bacon ragout with rosemary, 90
capers, simple spaghetti with olives and, 20
cardamom and orange buttered rice, 22
carrots: sweet steamed baby carrots with orange and coriander, 34
celery salad, crunchy, 99
cheese: aubergine steaks with feta salad, 71
feta, onion, parsley and lemon pizza topping, 99
Gorgonzola and walnut bread, 99
Gruyère dumplings, 92
mozzarella, pine nuts, capers and basil pizza topping, 98–9
Parmesan and Gruyère soufflés, 109
Parmesan cheese shavings, 11
penne with cheese, Parma ham, spinach and rocket, 20
rocket, bresaola and Parmesan pizza topping, 98
Roquefort sauce, 145
see also goats' cheese
cheese (soft): hot boozy berry puddings, 72
peach Marsala trifle, 146
sweet blueberry and cinnamon frittata with maple syrup, 111
warm chunky fish pâté, 39
cherries: cherry and cinnamon scones, 100
cherry almond tart, 149
chicken: charred paprika chicken, 76
chicken korma with almonds and cream, 88–9
coq au vin, 130
hot chicken tikka platter with yoghurt, 46
lemon spatchcocked chicken, 71
Mexican chicken burgers, 128
miso chicken broth with noodles, 120
roasting, 79
whole roasted chicken with prunes and thyme, 83
wholegrain mustard tarragon chicken, 29
chickpeas: luxury hoummus, 143
chicory, endive and radicchio salad with walnut dressing, 117
chillies: barbecued corn with chilli butter, 68
chile con carne wraps, 136
chilli sauce, 57
chillied chive egg noodles, 21
chunky guacamole, 143
hot wok chilli prawns with cucumber coriander salsa, 43–5
chips: root vegetable chunky chips with coriander mayo, 59

chives: chillied chive egg noodles, 21
chocolate: brandied hot chocolate, 156
hot chocolate fondue, 153
orange and bitter chocolate muffins, 96–7
pecan mocha brownies, 153
saucy chocolate pots, 39
brandied truffle curls, 153
chowder, watercress and bacon, 120
chutney, hot tomato and basil, 109
coconut cream: coconut and lime ice cream, 150
coconut milk: green Thai vegetable curry, 90
Thai fish broth, 27–8
cod: saffron fish roast, 84
coffee: amaretto iced cappuccino, 156
caffè frappè, 156
Irish coffee, 156
peach Marsala trifle, 146
coq au vin, 130
coriander leaves: coriander mayo, 59
coriander seeds: lamb steaks with coriander cumin crust, 64
corn cobs: barbecued corn with chilli butter, 68
courgettes: courgette quiche with sun-dried tomatoes, 106
herbed seared lamb with aubergine and courgette butter, 135
crab: warm Thai crab rice noodles, 21
cranberries: sea breeze, 157
venison sausages with port and cranberry ragout, 76
cucumber coriander salsa, hot wok chilli prawns with, 43–5
cumin: lamb steaks with coriander cumin crust, 64
lemon and cumin cracked wheat, 141
curries: chicken korma with almonds and cream, 88–9
green Thai vegetable curry, 90
hot chicken tikka platter with yoghurt, 46

D

deep-frying, 55–9
desserts, 146–153
brandied truffle curls, 153
cherry almond tart, 149
coconut and lime ice cream, 150
crusted lime polenta cake, 100
hot boozy berry puddings, 72
hot chocolate fondue, 153
hot tropical fruit parcels, 149
hot whisky pancakes with raspberries, 150
lime and ginger honey puddings, 34
mini pavlovas with hot sugared plums, 146
peach marsala trifle, 146
pecan mocha brownies, 153
plum clafoutis, 110
saucy chocolate pots, 39
sweet blueberry and cinnamon frittata with maple syrup, 111
Dijon dressing, 145
drinks, 154–7
duck: honeyed duck with mango salsa, 133
dumplings, Gruyère, 92

E

eggs, 105–11
poaching, 25

quails' eggs with three salts, **105**
rocket eggs with salsa verde, **105**
separating, **110**
sweet blueberry and cinnamon frittata with maple
   syrup, **111**
**endive, chicory and radicchio salad with walnut
   dressing, 117**

F
feta, onion, parsley and lemon pizza topping, **99**
fish and seafood, 123–7
   preparing, **124**
   steaming, **31**
   see also cod; salmon etc
fishcakes, trout, **126**
fondue, hot chocolate, **153**
food safety, 11
French beans: hot chicken tikka platter with yoghurt, **46**
**French toast with smoky bacon and spiked
   tomatoes, 108–9**
frittata: sweet blueberry and cinnamon frittata with
   maple syrup, **111**
fruit: fresh fruit for pudding, **150**
   hot boozy berry puddings, **72**
   hot chocolate fondue, **153**
   hot tropical fruit parcels, **149**
   very berry smoothie, **154**
frying, 49–53
   deep-frying, **55–9**
   stir-frying, **41–7**

G
garlic: crushed herb mash, **17**
   fried tomatoes with green pistou, **52**
   quick aioli, **144**
   steamed mussels with garlic and vermouth in a
      foil parcel, **34**
ginger: lime and ginger honey puddings, **32–3**
goats' cheese: pan-grilled bruschetta with red onion
      marmalade and goats' cheese, **64**
   peppered goats' cheese, **114**
Gorgonzola and walnut bread, 99
goulash, vegetable, **141**
green minestrone, 119
green Thai vegetable curry, 90
gremolata pork with lemon spinach, 52
grilling, 75–7
   barbecues, **67–73**
   grill pans, **61–5**
Gruyère dumplings, 92
guacamole, chunky **143**

H
**herbed seared lamb with aubergine and courgette
   butter, 135**
herby potato rösti, 51
honey: honey teriyaki vegetables, **43**
   honeyed duck with mango salsa, **133**
   lime and ginger honey puddings, **32–3**
horseradish: horseradish mash, **17**
   seared peppered beef salad with horseradish
      dressing, **114**
hoummus, luxury, **143**

I
ice cream: amaretto iced cappuccino, **156**
   coconut and lime ice cream, **150**
ingredients, 9
Irish coffee, 156

K
kidney beans: chile con carne wraps, **136**

L
lamb: herbed seared lamb with aubergine and
      courgette butter, **135**
   lamb steaks with coriander cumin crust, **64**
   Moroccan lamb tagine, **92–3**
   roasting, **79**
lamb's lettuce: seared scallops with brittle Parma, **62**
leeks: mushroom, leek and thyme puff pies, **140**
   venison sausages with port and cranberry
      ragout, **76**
lemon: gremolata pork with lemon spinach, **52**
   lemon beurre blanc, **145**
   lemon and cumin cracked wheat, **141**
   lemon spatchcocked chicken, **71**
**lemongrass and rosemary risotto with orange
   roasted roots, 139**
lentils: smoky Puy lentils with balsamic vinegar and
      pancetta, **22**
lettuce: stir-fried pork in lettuce cups, **46**
lime: coconut and lime ice cream, **150**
   crusted lime polenta cake, **100**
   lime and ginger honey puddings, **32–3**

M
mangoes: honeyed duck with mango salsa, **133**
   tropical smoothie, **154**
margarita, 157
mayonnaise: coriander mayo, **59**
   quick aioli, **144**
meat, 135–7
   on the barbecue, **72**
   roasting, **79**
Mediterranean fish stew, 123
menu planning 10
meringues: mini pavlovas with hot sugared
      plums, **146**
Mexican chicken burgers, 128
microwaving, 37–9
mini pavlovas with hot sugared plums, 146
miso chicken broth with noodles, 120
monkfish: Mediterranean fish stew, **123**
Moroccan lamb tagine, 92–3
mozzarella, pine nuts, capers and basil pizza
      topping, **98–9**
muffins, orange and bitter chocolate, **96–7**
mushrooms: mushroom, leek and thyme
      puff pies, **140**
   wild mushroom soup with sour cream and
      chives, **119**
mussels: steamed mussels with garlic and vermouth
      in a foil parcel, **34**
   Mediterranean fish stew, **123**
mustard: Dijon dressing, **145**
   mustard mash, **17**
   wholegrain mustard tarragon chicken, **29**

N
new potato salad with gazpacho dressing, 18
noodles: boiling, **21**
   Californian tuna noodle salad, **124**
   chillied chive egg noodles, **21**
   miso chicken broth with noodles, **120**
   warm Thai crab rice noodles, **21**
nuts, toasting, **11**

O
olives: black olive pizza crust, **98**
   simple spaghetti with capers and olives, **20**
   tomato tapenade salad, **113**
orange: orange and bitter chocolate muffins, **96–7**
   orange roasted roots, **84**
   sweet steamed baby carrots with orange and
      coriander, **34**

P
pancakes: hot whisky pancakes with raspberries, **150**
pancetta: hot crunchy croutons with smoked bacon
      and avocado, **113**
   smoky Puy lentils with balsamic vinegar and
      pancetta, **22**
par-boiling, 15
Parma ham: penne with cheese, Parma ham,
      spinach and rocket, **20**
   seared scallops with brittle Parma, **62**
Parmesan and Gruyère soufflés, 109
parsnips, creamy scalloped potatoes and, **139**
pasta: boiling, **20**
   penne with cheese, Parma ham, spinach and
      rocket, **20**
   peppered sage pork with pasta, **136**
pâté, warm chunky fish, **39**
pavlovas with hot sugared plums, 146
peach Marsala trifle, 146
pecan mocha brownies, 153
**penne with cheese, Parma ham, spinach and
   rocket, 20**
peppered goats' cheese, 114
peppers: fresh red pepper jam, **144**
   peppered sage pork with pasta, **136**
   pimento paste, **144–5**
   rich red pepper and bean soup, **121**
   simple grilled peppers, **77**
   smoky Puy lentils with balsamic vinegar and
      pancetta, **22**
pies: mushroom, leek and thyme puff pies, **140**
pimento paste, 144–5
pine nuts: broccoli trees with pan-fried pine nuts, **39**
   mozzarella, pine nuts, capers and basil pizza
      topping, **98–9**
pistou: fried tomatoes with green pistou, **52**
pizzas: black olive pizza crust, **98**
   toppings, **98–9**
plums: mini pavlovas with hot sugared plums, **146**
   plum clafoutis, **110**
poaching: 25–9
   in coconut milk, **27**
   in stock, **29**
polenta cake, crusted lime, **100**
popovers, salami and thyme, **110**
pork: gremolata pork with lemon spinach, **52**

159

peppered sage pork with pasta, **136**
roast loin of pork with butter-baked apples, **80**
roasting, **79**
stir-fried pork in lettuce cups, **46**
port and cranberry ragout, venison sausages with, **76**
potatoes: classic creamy mashed potatoes, **16**
creamy scalloped potatoes and parsnips, **139**
crushed herb mash, **17**
flavoured mashed potatoes, **17**
herby potato rösti, **51**
horseradish mash, **17**
mashed potato tips **17**
mustard mash, **17**
new potato salad with gazpacho dressing, **18**
roasted potatoes, **83**
seared peppered beef salad with horseradish
dressing, **114**
sun-dried tomato mash, **17**
trout fishcakes, **126**
watercress and bacon chowder, **120**
poussins with citrus baked rice, 133
prawns: barbecued steak with sizzled prawns, **72**
hot wok chilli prawns with cucumber coriander
salsa, **43–5**
Mediterranean fish stew, **123**
Thai fish broth, **27–8**
prunes, whole roasted chicken with thyme and, **83**
puddings: *see desserts*

Q
quails' eggs with three salts, 105
quiches: courgette quiche with sun-dried
tomatoes, **106**
smoked salmon and dill quiche, **106**

R
radicchio, endive and chicory salad with walnut
dressing, **117**
raspberries: hot whisky pancakes with, **150**
sweet tea-time bruschetta, **65**
red onion marmalade, 145
refreshing, 15
rice: boiling, **22**
cardamom and orange buttered rice, **22**
lemongrass and rosemary risotto with orange
roasted roots, **139**
poussins with citrus baked rice, **133**
roasting, 79–85
rocket: penne with cheese, Parma ham, spinach and
rocket, **20**
rocket, bresaola and Parmesan pizza topping, **98**
rocket eggs with salsa verde, **105**
rocket salsa verde, **143**
root vegetable chunky chips with coriander mayo, 59
Roquefort sauce, 145
rösti, herby potato, **51**

S
saffron fish roast, 84
salads, 113–17
aubergine steaks with feta salad, **71**
Californian tuna noodle salad, **124**
crunchy celery salad, **99**
endive, chicory and radicchio salad with walnut

dressing, **117**
hot crunchy croutons with smoked bacon and
avocado, **113**
new potato salad with gazpacho dressing, **18**
peppered goats' cheese, **114**
seared peppered beef salad with horseradish
dressing, **114**
tomato tapenade salad, **113**
tuna carpaccio salad, **117**
washing and drying salad leaves, **117**
salami and thyme popovers, 110
salmon: marinated vodka salmon, **125**
saffron fish roast, **84**
salmon tempura, **57–8**
Thai fish broth, **27–8**
warm chunky fish pâté, **39**
salsas: cucumber coriander salsa, **43–5**
honeyed duck with mango salsa, **133**
rocket eggs with salsa verde, **105**
rocket salsa verde, **143**
seared swordfish with avocado and salsa, **71**
salt: quails' eggs with three salts, **105**
sangría, 157
sauces: chilli sauce, **57**
Roquefort sauce, **145**
sausages: venison sausages with port and cranberry
ragout, **76**
scallops: seared scallops with brittle Parma, **62**
scones, cherry and cinnamon, **100**
sea breeze, 157
seafood and fish: 123–7
cooking and preparing, **124**
separating eggs, 110
smoked salmon and dill quiche, 106
smoothies, 154
soufflés, Parmesan and Gruyère, **109**
soups, 119–21
green minestrone, **119**
miso chicken broth with noodles, **120**
rich red pepper and bean soup, **121**
Thai fish broth, **27–8**
watercress and bacon chowder, **120**
wild mushroom soup with sour cream and
chives, **119**
spaghetti: green minestrone, **119**
simple spaghetti with capers and olives, **20**
spinach: gremolata pork with lemon spinach, **52**
hot chicken tikka platter with yoghurt, **46**
penne with cheese, Parma ham, spinach and
rocket, **20**
spring vegetable vinaigrette, 18
steamed puddings: lime and ginger honey
puddings, **32–3**
steaming, 31–5
stir-frying, 41–7
strawberries: sweet tea-time bruschetta, **65**
swordfish: seared swordfish with avocado and salsa,
71

T
tagine, Moroccan lamb, **92–3**
tapenade: tomato tapenade salad, **113**
tart, cherry almond, **149**
teacakes: sweet tea-time bruschetta, **65**

tempura, salmon, **57–8**
tequila: margarita, **157**
teriyaki vegetables, 43
Thai crab rice noodles, 21
Thai fish broth, 27–8
toasting nuts and seeds, 11
tomatoes: bean and bacon ragout with rosemary, **90**
bloody Mary, **157**
chunky guacamole, **143**
courgette quiche with sun-dried tomatoes, **106**
deseeding, **11**
French toast with smoky bacon and spiked
tomatoes, **108–9**
fried tomatoes with green pistou, **52**
hot tomato and basil chutney, **109**
new potato salad with gazpacho dressing, **18**
seared peppered beef salad with horseradish
dressing, **114**
sun-dried tomato mash, **17**
tomato tapenade salad, **113**
tortillas: chile con carne wraps, **136**
trifle, peach Marsala, **146**
tropical fruit parcels, 149
tropical smoothie, 154
trout: trout fishcakes, **126**
trout with tarragon and bacon, **68**
tuna: Californian tuna noodle salad, **124**
tuna carpaccio salad, **117**

V
vegetables, 139–41
green minestrone, **119**
green Thai vegetable curry, **90**
honey teriyaki vegetables, **43**
lemongrass and rosemary risotto with orange
roasted roots, **139**
orange roasted roots, **84**
roasting, **84**
root vegetable chunky chips with coriander mayo, **59**
saffron fish roast, **84**
spring vegetable vinaigrette, **18**
vegetable goulash, **141**
venison sausages with port and cranberry ragout, 76
very berry smoothie, 154
vinaigrette, spring vegetable, **18**
vodka: bloody Mary, **157**
marinated vodka salmon, **125**
sea breeze, **157**

W
walnuts: Gorgonzola and walnut bread, **99**
watercress and bacon chowder, 120
whisky pancakes with raspberries, 150
whiskey: Irish coffee, **156**
wine: sangría, **157**
woks: 41
steaming fish in a wok, **34**

Y
yoghurt: hot chicken tikka platter with yoghurt, **46**
lamb steaks with coriander cumin crust, **64**
Roquefort sauce, **145**
very berry smoothie, **154**
warm chunky fish pâté, **39**